ON THE BORDERLANDS OF GREAT EMPIRES

Transylvanian Armies 1541–1613

Florin Nicolae Ardelean

‘

Helion & Company

Helion & Company Limited
Unit 8 Amherst Business Centre
Budbrooke Road
Warwick
CV34 5WE
England
Tel. 01926 499 619
Email: info@helion.co.uk
Website: www.helion.co.uk
Twitter: @helionbooks
Visit our blog http://blog.helion.co.uk/

Published by Helion & Company 2022
Designed and typeset by Serena Jones
Cover designed by Paul Hewitt, Battlefield Design (www.battlefield-design.co.uk)

Cover: Mounted soldier from the court army (guard) of Prince Sigismund Báthory/Hajdú soldier from
the western borderlands of Transylvania during the Long Turkish War (1591–1606), illustration by Cătălin
Drăghici © Helion & Company 2022

ISBN 978-1-914059-69-8

British Library Cataloguing-in-Publication Data.
A catalogue record for this book is available from the British Library.

For details of other military history titles published by Helion & Company
Limited, contact the above address, or visit our website: http://www.helion.co.uk

We always welcome receiving book proposals from prospective authors.

Contents

Introduction

Transylvania Before the Age of the Principality

Transylvania is a historical region in east-central Europe, today part of Romania. Positioned in the eastern half of the Carpathian Basin, Transylvania is surrounded by mountains on all sides. In time, some neighbouring regions situated beyond the western Carpathians were also associated with Transylvania. The north-western Banat and the so-called *Partium* region (*Partes Regni Hungariae*), consisting of several counties from the eastern half of the medieval Kingdom of Hungary, became an integral part of the Transylvanian Principality during the second half of the sixteenth century.

In ancient times, the region that was later called Transylvania was inhabited by Dacians. Scythian, Celtic, Illyrian and Sarmatian groups were also identified in written sources or by archaeological excavations as inhabiting this region. During the first century BC, Burebista created a vast kingdom that included the Dacian tribes and the other peoples from the Eastern Carpathian Basin. It was most likely a loose tribal union, but it was powerful enough to attract the attention of Europe's mightiest political and military power at the time; Rome. The conflict between the two states began in 86 AD. After a few decades of intermittent warfare, the Romans were able to expand their dominion beyond the Danube. The decisive blow against the Kingdom of Dacia, ruled by Decebal, was delivered by the Roman Emperor Trajan, who organised two campaigns against his northern neighbour in 101–102 AD and 105–106 AD.

After the military conquest, a large part of the former Dacian kingdom was organised as a province of the Roman Empire. For more than one and a half centuries (from 106 to 271 AD) the regions encompassed by the Carpathians and the lower course of the Danube were part of the Roman world. Dacians, Romans and colonists of various origins brought from other Roman provinces lived together on the north-eastern edges of the Empire. In 271 AD, due to repeated attacks from the neighbouring barbarian tribes, Emperor Aurelian decided to withdraw from Dacia. The Imperial administration and the army were moved south of the Danube in order to organise a more efficient defence along the course of the river.

Over the following seven centuries, during the so-called Migration Period, the territory which will be later identified as Transylvania was part of the ephemeral states organised by several migrating populations. Goths,

Huns, Gepids, Avars, Slavs and Bulgarians exercised temporary control over this region, until the Hungarian conquest began.

The Hungarians (Magyars) settled in Pannonia at the end of the ninth century. Once established in their new home, their leaders expanded the boundaries of the kingdom by occupying several neighbouring regions. In the east they conquered Transylvania, reaching the Carpathian mountains, which represented an easily defensible natural obstacle. The Hungarian occupation of Transylvania was a long process that ended in the thirteenth century. The name of this historical region, Transylvania, dates from this period, and it first had a slightly different form, *Terra Ultrasilvana*, meaning 'the land beyond the forest'.[1] The name was also used in connection to one of the early rulers of this region, *Mercurius princeps ultrasilvanus*, in documents issued in 1111 and 1113.[2] However, Transylvania became the name most commonly used with its various forms in the languages of the most numerous ethnic groups inhabiting the region: *Transilvania* (Romanian), *Erdély* (Hungarian) and *Siebenbürgen* (German).

For about five centuries Transylvania was a voivodeship (a form of territorial organisation specific to Romanian and Slavic populations) within the borders of the Hungarian Kingdom. In 1526, the Hungarian army was soundly defeated by the army of the Ottoman sultan, Suleiman the Magnificent, at the battle of Mohács. During the following decades the lands that were once part of the Hungarian Crown were divided. On the eastern parts of the former Hungarian kingdom a new state was born, the Principality of Transylvania. For one and a half centuries (1541–1691), Transylvania was a distinct state on the maps of Europe, and played an important military and strategic role in the struggle between the Ottomans and the Habsburgs in central and south-east Europe.

---

1   Alexandru Madgearu, *The Romanians in the Anonymous Gesta Hungarorum: Truth and Fiction* (Cluj-Napoca: Romanian Cultural Institute, 2005), p.85.

2   Thomas Nägler, 'Transylvania between 900 and 1300', in Ioan-Aurel Pop, Thomas Nägler (eds), *The History of Transylvania* (Cluj-Napoca: Centre for Transylvanian Studies. Romanian Cultural Institute, 2005), vol. I, p.217; László Makkai, 'Transylvania in the Medieval Hungarian Kingdom', in Béla Köpeczi (ed.), *History of Transylvania* (New York: Columbia University Press, 2001), vol. I, p.407.

Note on Personal and Place Names

Due to the complex ethnic composition of east-central European regions, places and historical personalities have various names in different languages. For the sake of readability and comprehension I have decided to use English versions for first names of rulers or other important personalities like John Sigismund Szapolyai, Stephen Báthory or George Martinuzzi. For other personal names I have kept the version in their native language or how they appear in contemporary sources, such as Menyhért Balassa or Giovanni Battista Castaldo. For names of places (countries, regions and towns) I have chosen the English versions where such an equivalent exists; Transylvania, Poland, Vienna etc. In all other situation I have decided to use the modern names for easier identification, for example, Košice (instead of Kassa or Cassovia) or Timișoara (instead of Temesvár or Temeschwar).

1

The Birth of the Transylvanian Principality

From Voivode to Prince – the Rulers of Transylvania (1541–1613)

The formation of the Transylvanian Principality was a rather long historical process, lasting several decades. Many historians consider the year 1541, marked by the Ottoman conquest of Buda, as a starting point. The fall of the royal seat of the Hungarian kings lead to an effective division of the kingdom into three parts: the central and southern parts of the former kingdom became provinces of the Ottoman Empire, the western and northern regions were taken by the Habsburgs who claimed the right to inherit the Hungarian Crown and the eastern parts were gradually transformed into a new state, under Ottoman suzerainty, later known as the Principality of Transylvania.

The entire political history of Transylvania during the early modern period was marked by the confrontation between the Ottomans and the Habsburgs. The Transylvanian Principality survived for as long as it did, because its rulers were able to take advantage of the shifting balance of power between these two empires.

After the battle of Mohács (1526), most of the eastern parts of the Hungarian kingdom, including Transylvania, acknowledged the rule of John Szapolyai and his pro-Ottoman policy. The King died on 22 July 1540, in the camp of his army, near Sebeş, while he was taking action against a rebellious Transylvanian faction led by Stephen Mailat. The elderly King had recently received the joyful news that his wife, Isabella, daughter of the Polish King Sigismund I Jagiellon, had given birth to a son, John Sigismund. Until his coming of age, the country was ruled by a group of councillors. Among them the most influential were his mother, Queen Isabella Jagiellon, and the Bishop of Oradea, George Martinuzzi (Juraj Utiešenović). A Pauline friar who had previously held the position of treasurer under King John, Martinuzzi was the most powerful dignitary in the eastern parts of the former

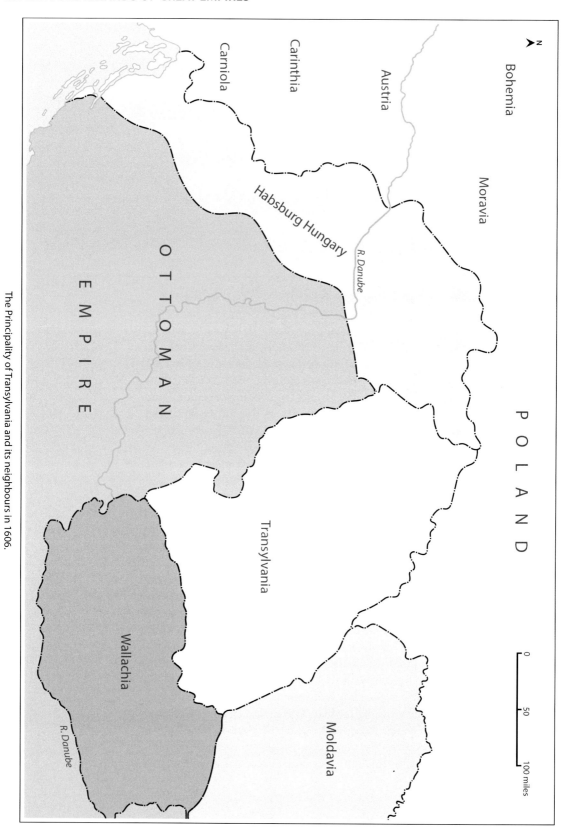

The Principality of Transylvania and its neighbours in 1606.

Hungarian kingdom, who played a decisive role in the formation of the Transylvanian Principality.[1]

The representatives of the counties, seats and districts situated on the eastern side of the Tisza River assembled separately for the first time in 1541, in the market town of Debrecen. They pledged loyalty to the son of King John Szapolyai, John Sigismund, and accepted Ottoman suzerainty. As vassals of the sultan, the Transylvanians had to pay a tribute (initially 10,000 florins) and provide military assistance when the Ottomans requested it.[2]

In 1542 Martinuzzi was acknowledged as governor of Transylvania. In the following years he negotiated with both the Habsburgs and the Ottomans in order to secure the survival of the new-born state. At the same time, representatives of the Transylvanian estates (Nobles, Saxons and Székely) invited Queen Isabella and her infant son to reside in Transylvania. The royal family moved from Lipova, an estate of the Szapolyai family on the south-western sector of the Transylvanian frontier, to Alba Iulia, residence of the Bishop of Transylvania.[3]

In the following years, a bitter rivalry developed between Queen Isabella and the manipulative bishop who acted as a true monarch. Deeply disappointed by this situation, the young and inexperienced Queen expressed her willingness to give up the throne in favour of the Habsburgs. The first negotiations began in 1548 but Isabella hesitated. In the meantime Martinuzzi kept contacts with the Habsburgs and promised to acknowledge their rule in exchange for the title of governor and a position of cardinal. The tension between the opposing factions reached a climax in 1550 when a civil war broke out. The Habsburgs were able to gain the upper hand when they sent an army of about 7,000 mercenaries to Transylvania, under the command of Giovanni Battista Castaldo.[4]

From 1551 to 1556 Transylvania was under the control of the Habsburgs. Isabella and her son left Transylvania and sought refuge at the Polish royal court. General Castaldo and his troops were stationed in the country until 1553.

John Sigismund Szapolyai, son of King John Szapolyai and ruler of the eastern parts of the Hungarian Kingdom (1559–1571).

---

1   On the origins and early career of this remarkable personality see Adriano Papo, Gizella Nemeth Papo, *Frate GiorgioMartinuzzi: Cardinale, soldato e statista dalmata agli albori del Principato di Transilvania* (Canterano: Arcane editrice, 2017), pp.21–111.

2   Cristina Feneşan, 'Le statut de dépendance de la principauté de Transylvanié envers la Porte en 1541', *Revue des études sud-est européennes*, XXXVII–XXXVIII (1999–2000), pp.79–91.

3   László Makkai, 'The first period of the Principality of Transylvania (1526–1606)', in Béla Köpeczi (ed.), *History of Transylvania*, vol. I (New York: Columbia University Press, 2001), p.614.

4   Florin Nicolae Ardelean, 'On the Foreign Mercenaries and Early Modern Military Innovations in East Central Europe. The Army Castaldo in Transylvania and the Banat 1551–1553', in György Bujdosné Pap, Ingrid Fejér, Ágota H. Szilasi (eds), *Mozgó Frontvonalak. Háború és diplomácia a várháborúk időszakában 1552–1568, Studia Agriensia*, 35 (Eger: Dobó István Vármúzeum, 2017), pp.117–128.

During this period, the Habsburg military commander shared authority with Andrew Báthory, count of Satu-Mare and Szabolcs, and Thomas Nádasdy, who was residing in the fortress of Făgăraş, on the southern Transylvanian border.[5] George Martinuzzi maintained many political and administrative prerogatives until 16 December 1551, when he was assassinated by the soldiers of Castaldo. This act was carried out with the approval of the Habsburg Emperor who was afraid that the ambitious clergyman would betray him and join the Ottomans.[6] The soldiers of Castado in Transylvania were considered by a contemporary observer to be 'too small for an army, too large for a diplomatic mission'.[7] They were unable to withstand the Ottoman offensive in the Banat region and the important fortress of Timişoara was lost in 1552. During the following year the Habsburg mercenary army was withdrawn from Transylvania because their presence was antagonising the local population. In May 1553 Emperor Ferdinand I appointed two voivodes, Francis Kendi and Stephen Dobó,[8] one was a representative of the Transylvanian nobility while the other was a loyal noble and military commander from Royal Hungary. In spite of this attempt to restore order, the Habsburgs were gradually losing control over Transylvania.

As Ottoman military pressure increased, Queen Isabella and her son, John Sigismund, returned to Transylvania from their exile in Poland. On 22 October 1556, they reached the town of Cluj and soon after they summoned the Diet in order to re-establish their authority.[9] Most of the nobility and the other estates pledged their loyalty to House Szapolyai once again and were prepared to expel the remaining Habsburg troops from the country. The conflict with the Habsburgs lasted for about fifteen years, until the peace treaty of Speyer was ratified in 1571. During this period there was no proper border between Transylvania and Royal Hungary in the Upper Tisza region. The nobility from the area regularly shifted their allegiance between the two rulers, one residing in Vienna, the other in Alba Iulia. The Habsburg–Transylvanian conflict coincided roughly with a new Ottoman offensive in Hungary known as the 'Fortress War' (1552–1568). Most Transylvanian military campaigns were coordinated with Turkish attacks on some of the most important strategic points on the Hungarian frontier.

In 1559, on 15 November, Queen Isabella Jagiellon died, and John Sigismund assumed effective leadership of Transylvania, although he still claimed the title of King of Hungary. His entire reign was marked by conflict with the Habsburgs. The campaigns organised during these years had a crucial role in redefining the military organisation of Transylvania. John Sigismund had to mobilise the human and material resources of his country in a war against a far superior opponent, the Habsburgs. Although

---

5   Österreichisches Staatsarchiv, Haus-Hof und Staatsarchiv, Vienna, Hungarica, Algemeine Akten (ÖStA, HHStA, Hungarica AA), Fas. 57, Konv. A, pp.50–52.

6   Papo, Nemeth Papo, *Frate Giorgio*, pp.266–292.

7   Ascanio Centorio degli Hortensii, *Comentarii della guerra di Transilvania* (Vinegia: Appresso Gabriel Giolito de' Ferrari, 1565), p.68.

8   Zsigmond Jákó, 'Despre numirea voievozilor Transilvaniei', *Acta Musei Napocensis*, 26–30, (1994) doc. 6, pp.43–44.

9   *Monumenta Comitialia Regni Transylvaniae* (*MCRT*), Sándor Szilágyi (ed.), vol. II (Budapest: Magyar Tudományos Akad. Könyvkiadó Hivatala, 1876), p.53.

he benefited from direct or indirect Ottoman military help, John Sigismund was unable to achieve significant success on the battlefield. In 1561 he lost most of the territories in the Upper Tisza region when Menyhért Balassa betrayed him and joined the Habsburgs. One year later, on the 4 March 1562, he lost the most important pitched battle of this war, at Hodod, and had to deal with a major rebellion of the Székely. In this context John Sigismund became aware of the importance of Ottoman protection and decided to visit Sultan Süleyman the Magnificent in 1566, while he was personally leading the Ottoman army in Hungary. The Sultan died the same year while his troops were besieging Szigetvár. Selim II, his successor, reached a peace agreement with the Habsburgs in 1568. This radical change of context determined John Sigismund to cease hostilities and begin negotiations with the Habsburgs. The peace treaty was signed at Speyer, in 1570. John Sigismund gave up the title of King of Hungary and officially assumed the title of Prince. Another important consequence of this peace treaty was the establishment of a clear border between Transylvania and Royal Hungary. The counties of Maramureş, Crasna, Middle Solnoc and Bihor were acknowledged as Transylvanian territory, while the other disputed counties in the East Tisza region remained part of Royal Hungary.[10]

John Sigismund was unable to enjoy the results of his political and military efforts because he died on 14 March 1571. A few months later, on 25 May, the Transylvanian Diet chose a new ruler, Stephen Báthory. Although not all Transylvanian estates were satisfied with this choice, they expressed no objection when the majority decided that Báthory was best suited for the position of voivode.[11] In March 1572, Sultan Selim II formally recognised Stephen Báthory as ruler of Transylvania. A fundamental principle of Transylvanian statehood was thus established; the free election of the ruling prince followed by the recognition of the Porte. Stephen Báthory was the wealthiest and most influential representative of the local nobility. He was educated in Padua and had accumulated significant military and political experience during the reign of his predecessor.[12] In the first years of his reign, Báthory had to deal with his rival Gaspar Bekes. The quarrelsome noble held control over Făgăraş, the most important fortification on the southern border of Transylvania. The legitimate voivode besieged Făgăraş in 1573 but Bekes managed to escape and sought refuge in the lands of the Habsburgs. He returned two years later, in 1575, with an army of mercenaries gathered with Habsburg support. Stephen Báthory faced him on the battlefield of Sânpaul and managed to win a decisive victory that consolidated his reign in Transylvania and increased his reputation among the neighbouring countries.[13]

---

10   Imre Lukinich, *Erdély területi változásai a török hódítás korában, 1541–1711* (Budapest: Kiadja a Magyar Tudományos Akadémia, 1918), pp.129–131.

11   Felicia Roşu, *Elective Monarchy in Transylvania and Poland-Lithuania, 1569–1587* (Oxford University Press, 2017), pp.101–103.

12   Imre Lukinich, 'La jeunesse d'Etienne Báthory', in Adrien de Divéky (ed.), *Etienne Báthory: roi de Pologne, prince de Transylvanie* (Cracow, 1935), pp.23–34.

13   Sándor Szilágyi, 'Békés Gáspár versengése Báthori Istvánnal (1571–1575)', *Erdélyi Múzeum-Egyesület Évkönyve*, I (1859–1861), pp.107–115.

STEPHANVS BATHORIVS WEIWODEN AVS SIEBNBVRGEN M.D.LXXVI.

Stephen Báthory, voivode of Transylvania (1571–1576) and King of the Polish-Lithuanian Commonwealth (1576–1586).

Stephen Báthory was elected king of the Polish-Lithuanian Commonwealth on 15 December 1575. His marriage to Anna Jagiellon was a decisive factor in the choice expressed by the members of the Sejm (the Polish-Lithuanian estates assembly).[14] In the spring of 1576, Báthory travelled to Poland and left his brother, Christopher Báthory, in charge of Transylvanian affairs. In the following years Christopher ruled Transylvania as voivode, but he always acted as a representative of his brother. After his death in 1581, his son, Sigismund, was chosen as voivode. The young and inexperienced ruler lacked real authority and, until 1586, all important decisions regarding Transylvania were made by his uncle, the King of Poland. When Stephen Báthory died in 1586, Sigismund inherited his rule over Transylvania.

The Transylvanian estates gained considerable authority and refused to recognise Sigismund as legitimate ruler until 1588, when he agreed to expel the Jesuits from the country. A large proportion of the Transylvanian elite had chosen various Protestant confessions (Lutheran, Calvinist, and Unitarian) and were feeling threatened by a revival of the Catholic Church.[15] However, the young Prince (he was only 16 in 1588) was slowly building a network of trusted nobles, among whom a prominent figure was his uncle, Stephen Bocskai, who helped him take full authority in the following years.

In 1591 border conflicts between the Ottomans and the Habsburgs reached a high level of intensity. The two empires were about to engage in an open conflict, known as the Long Turkish War, which would last 15 years, until 1606. Transylvania was unable to avoid this war and the political elite of the country was divided between those who favoured the Ottomans and those who were tempted to join the Holy League. The 'Ottoman faction' held a majority in the Diet and was able to postpone a direct involvement in the first years of the conflict. The young and ambitious Prince Sigismund Báthory had other plans and wanted to join the Holy League. The Diet, assembled in Turda on 12 May 1594, refused to support the Prince in a war against the Ottomans, but Transylvanian troops had already been in action in the Banat region supporting the Serbian uprising.[16] The Transylvanian Prince

---

14 Louis Szádeczky, 'L'election d'Etienne Báthory au trône de Pologne', in Adrien de Divéky (ed.), *Etienne Báthory: roi de Pologne, prince de Transylvanie* (Cracow, 1935), pp.82–105.

15 Makkai, '*The first period of the Principality*', pp.744–745.

16 Cristina Feneșan, 'Din premisele luptei antiotomane a Țărilor Române în vremea lui Mihai Viteazul. Mișcările populare din 1594 în eialetul Timișoarei', *Anuarul Institutului de Istorie și Arheologie Cluj-Napoca*, XXVII, (1985–1986), pp.100–116.

was unable to pursue his strategic objectives due to lack of internal support. In August 1594 Sigismund summoned the Diet in the town of Cluj. Unaware of his true intentions, the nobles who favoured Ottoman vassalage came without taking any precautions. With the help of his loyal supporters and the soldiers from his personal guard, Prince Sigismund managed to eliminate the opposition in one night. He imprisoned and executed most of the leaders, including his cousin Balthazar Báthory.[17] During the same year, the Transylvanian Prince concluded alliances with Michael the Brave, ruler of Wallachia, and Aron Vodă, ruler of Moldavia, strengthening his position against the Ottomans. The two Romanian voivodes became vassals of Sigismund.

Transylvania joined the war under very good conditions. The Prince managed to gain the full support of the estates and was able to build strong alliances with his closest neighbours, Wallachia and Moldavia. In March 1595, Sigismund signed a new agreement with the Habsburgs and married the archduchess, Maria Christierna. In autumn he led a successful campaign in Wallachia that ended with the capture of the Giurgiu fortress on the Danube.

Sigismund Báthory, Prince of Transylvania (1588–1601).

However, the situation changed drastically the following year. It all began with a new rebellion of the Székely that was violently suppressed. The event would be later recorded in chronicles as the 'Bloody Carnival'.[18] In the summer of 1596 Sigismund personally commanded the Transylvanian army in an attempt to retake Timişoara, which had become the centre of an Ottoman province (*villayet*) after 1552. The Transylvanians suffered a bitter defeat and were forced to abandon their ambitious objective. In the meantime a large Ottoman army, led by Sultan Mehmet III himself was advancing towards the Habsburg border. Sigismund Báthory was summoned to fulfil his duties as a member of the Holly League and joined the army of the Habsburgs. A major pitched battle took place on the fields of Mezőkeresztes, on 23–26 October 1596. The Ottomans were victorious but were unable to radically shift the balance of the war.[19]

---

17 Andrei Veress (ed.), *Documente privitoare la istoria Ardealului, Moldovei şi Ţării Româneşti, Acte şi scrisori,* vol. IV, 1932, doc. 70, pp.123–125.

18 *Memorialul lui Nagy Szabó Ferencz din Târgu Mureş (1580–1658)*, Ştefania Gáll Mihăilescu (ed.) (Bucureşti, 1993), pp.78–80.

19 András Komáromy, 'A Mezőkeresztesi csata 1596-ban', *Hadtörténelmi Közlemények*, V (1892), pp.278–298.

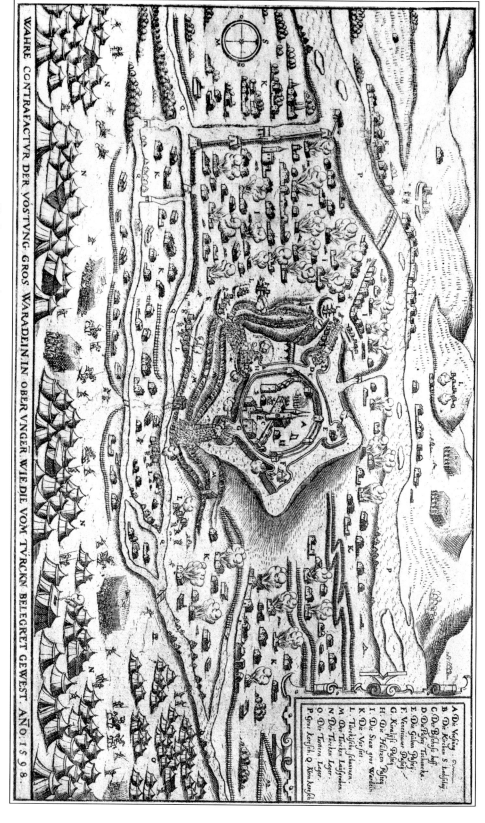

The Ottoman army besieging Oradea in 1598. (Ţării Crişurilor Museum, Oradea, România)

After a second failed attempt to conquer Timişoara in 1597, Sigismund Báthory lost confidence in his ability to rule Transylvania and in the chances of the Holy League to win the war. On 23 December 1597 he gave up the throne and retreated to Silesia. The Habsburg Emperor appointed three commissioners to govern Transylvania in his name: István Szuhay, Miklós Istvánffy and Bartholomeus Pezzen. The Transylvanian estates were not satisfied with this political solution. Stephen Bocskai and other nobles convinced Sigismund to return to Transylvania in August 1598 and led the country once again in the fight against the Ottomans. The situation had not changed very much but the Christian armies managed to obtain a significant victory in the autumn of 1598, when a mixed Habsburg–Transylvanian garrison repelled an Ottoman siege on the fortress of Oradea.[20]

On 17 March 1599, Prince Sigismund abdicated for the second time. His place was taken by his cousin, Cardinal Andrew Báthory. The new ruling Prince enjoyed excellent relations with the Polish-Lithuanian Commonwealth and his main objective was to end the Transylvanian involvement in the anti-Ottoman war. The members of the Holy League reacted with haste because they were unwilling to lose such an important ally. The Wallachian ruler, Michael the Brave, was the first who acted against the new Transylvanian leadership. His army began marching across the Carpathians in early October 1599. A few weeks later, on 28 October, he defeated the Transylvanian army at Şelimbăr, near the Saxon town of Sibiu. During the next months, Michael the Brave ruled Transylvania as a representative of the Habsburgs. He summoned three Diets during his short rule in an attempt to consolidate his position. He placed several Wallachian boyars in important military and administrative offices, and he issued some laws in favour of the Romanian and Orthodox population of Transylvania. He also secured the loyalty of the Székelys, who had their traditional privileges restored.[21] However, most of the nobility was unsatisfied with his rule. Soon, a strong opposition was formed around the influential noble Stephen Csáky, an initial supporter of the Romanian ruler and captain general of the Transylvanian army.[22]

The discontent noble faction joined forces with the Habsburg army, commanded by General Giorgio Basta,[23] and defeated Michael the Brave in the battle of Mirăslău, on 18 September 1600. General Basta governed Transylvania for the next four months. In February 1601 his authority was challenged by Sigismund Báthory who claimed, for the third time, the title of Transylvanian Prince, with Polish and Ottoman help. Emperor Rudolf

---

20 Doru Marta, *Cetatea Oradiei: De la începuturi până sfârşitul secolului al XVII–lea* (Oradea, 2013), p.49.

21 Ioachim Crăciun (ed.), 'Dietele Transilvaniei ţinute sub domnia lui Mihaiu Viteazul (1599–1600)', *Anuarul Institutului de Istorie Naţională Cluj*, VII (1936–1938), pp.620–640.

22 Florin Nicolae Ardelean, 'Evoluţia funcţiei de căpitan general în Transilvania la sfârşitul secolului al XVI–lea şi la în prima jumătate a secolului al XVII–lea', *Banatica*, 28 (2018), pp.563–566.

23 Giorgio Basta was a Habsburg commander of Albanian origin who had previously fought in the Spanish army of the Low Countries, see Zoltán Péter Bagi, 'Giorgio Basta: a short summary of a career', in Krisztián Csaplár-Degovics (ed.), *These were hard times for Skanderbeg, but he had an ally, the Hungarian Hunyadi: Episodes in Albanian–Hungarian Historical Contacts* (Budapest: Research Centre for the Humanities – Hungarian Academy of Sciences, 2019), pp.35–67.

Giorgio Basta (1550–1607), commander of Habsburg troops in Transylvania and eastern Hungary.

II was determined to keep Transylvania under his control and dispatched new troops and resources in this region. Michael the Brave and Giorgio Basta were reconciled and marched together against Sigismund who was now ruling Transylvania as a faithful Ottoman vassal. The two armies met on the battlefield of Guruslău where the Habsburgs won a new victory on 3 August 1601. After the battle, the Romanian voivode was assassinated by Walloon mercenaries who were following the orders of Basta. The Habsburg General suspected that Michael was in contact with the Turks and intended to betray the Holy League. These accusations were never convincingly proven.[24]

In 1602 Transylvania was overrun by foreign soldiers of various origins. While Giorgio Basta maintained control over the northern half of the country with his German, Italian and Walloon mercenaries, the southern half acknowledged the authority of Prince Sigismund aided by Polish, Wallachian, Moldavian, Ottoman and Tatar troops. A war of attrition between the two sides depleted the resources of the country and generated a constant state of insecurity among the population. Although Basta was forced to retreat, Prince Sigismund gave up the Transylvanian throne for the last time. He eventually died in exile, in Prague, in 1613.[25]

Throughout this long military conflict both Ottomans and Habsburgs were able to gain support among the Transylvanian ruling class. The lack of a common political orientation favoured the frequent change of leadership in Transylvania during the Long Turkish War. After Sigismund's final abdication, the Ottomans chose another candidate for the Transylvanian throne, Moses Székely, who was elected Prince on 8 May 1603. He was an influential noble hailing from the Székely Seat of Odorhei, with an impressive military carrier.[26] On 17 July 1603, the new Transylvanian Prince lost his life on a battlefield near Brașov, fighting against the Wallachian ruler, Radu Șerban. Once *again*, the Habsburgs had gained the upper hand and Basta returned to Transylvania as governor until 1604.

The last two years of the Long Turkish War were marked by the uprising of Stephen Bocskai against the Habsburg rule in Hungary. This rebellion was sparked by religious persecution against Protestants in Hungary, but the inability of the Habsburgs to conclude the conflict with the Ottomans was also an important factor. The hostilities began in Bihor County where Bocskai had his most important estates. By the end of the year 1604, the rebels were able to

24 Petre P. Panaitescu, *Mihai Viteazul* (București: Fundația Regele Carol I, 1936), pp.247–248.
25 Makkai, 'The first period of the Principality', p.757.
26 Ardelean, 'Evoluția funcției de căpitan general', pp.561–563.

capture Košice, the administrative and military centre of Upper Hungary.[27] Recognising a great opportunity to tip the scales of the war in his favour, Sultan Ahmed I acknowledged Bocskai as Prince of Transylvania. He was recognised by the Transylvanian Diet almost one year later, on 14 September 1605, at the Diet of Mediaş. By the end of 1605, Bocskai and his troops were in control of most of Royal Hungary. In November 1605, Bocskai was elected King of Hungary with Ottoman approval. During this period his involvement in Transylvanian affairs was minimal and his interests in the region were represented by his captain general, László Gyulaffi.[28] On 23 June 1606, Bocskai and the Habsburgs made peace. The treaty was signed in Vienna. The most important provisions regarding Transylvania established the frontier between the Principality and Royal Hungary. The north-western border of Transylvania was expanded and included the counties of Satu-Mare, Szabolcs, Ugocsa and Bereg. A few months later the Long Turkish War ended. On 15 November 1606, the two Empires signed the Peace Treaty of Zsitvatorok. Stephen Bocskai died in Košice, on 29 December 1606, at the age of 49.[29]

At the end of the war, the Principality of Transylvania had gained new territories but the social and economic impact of the conflict was devastating. Many consecutive years of warfare had disrupted economic activities. Trade was reduced and peasants were unable to regularly tend to their fields because they had to seek shelter when armies approached. Many foreign armies crossed the territories of the Principality during these years and, as was the custom in those days, each resorted to plundering. The chronicler István Szamosközy, an eyewitness of these events, has written about 'the eight consecutive destructions of Transylvania', referring to some of the most radical political and military changes that occurred during the last phase of the war.[30]

Stephen Bocskai, Prince of Transylvania and King of Hungary 1605–1606, *Trachten-Kabinett von Siebenbürgens*, 1729. (The National Museum of Transylvanian History, Cluj-Napoca, Romania)

27 Géza Pálffy, *The Kingdom of Hungary and the Habsburg Monarchy in the Sixteenth Century* (Boulder, Colorado: Social Science Monographs, 2009), pp.216–217.
28 Ardelean, 'Evoluţia funcţiei de căpitan general', pp.566–568.
29 Makkai, 'The first period of the Principality', pp.764–768.
30 Ioachim Crăciun (ed.), *Cronicarul Szamosközy şi însemnările lui privitoare la români 1566–1608* (Cluj: Institutul de Arte Grafice Ardealul, 1928), p.151.

Sigismund Rákóczy, Prince of Transylvania 1607–1608, *Trachten-Kabinett von Siebenbürgens*, 1729. (The National Museum of Transylvanian History, Cluj-Napoca, Romania)

In his testament, Stephen Bocskai had designated Bálint Hommonai, an important nobleman from Upper Hungary, as his successor. The Ottomans respected the wishes of the dead Prince and confirmed Hommonai as Transylvanian ruler. The estates were not content with this choice, because their right of free election was ignored. In this context they decided to give their support to a different candidate, Sigismund Rákóczy, who had actually ruled Transylvania as governor and captain general in 1606. The Diet assembled on 7 February 1607, elected Sigismund Rákóczy as Prince. Unwilling to generate further tension on the northern edges of his empire, the sultan gave up on his initial choice and acknowledged the candidate elected by the estates.[31] Rákóczy had an outstanding career, rising from the ranks of the lesser nobility to the Transylvanian throne. During his short rule (February 1607 to March 1608), he focused on rebuilding the country after the Long Turkish War by encouraging foreign trade and consolidating diplomatic relations with the neighbouring Romanian principalities, Moldavia and Wallachia.[32]

On 8 March 1608, Sigismund Rákóczy gave up the throne in favour of a younger candidate, Gabriel Báthory. A distant relative of the former prince, Sigismund Báthory, Gabriel managed to secure the support of the hajdús, a social and military category that thrived on the frontier area in Hungary and Transylvania. The hajdús were initially involved in cattle trading and they were located predominantly in the counties along the Tisza River. As the Ottoman threat increased, they also became very skilled in irregular warfare. They played a major military role during the rebellion of Stephen Bocskai (1604–1606) who had granted them collective privileges and tax exemptions.[33] They followed Báthory because they needed a protector, a strong leader who would guarantee their recently earned privileges.

Soon after he became ruler of Transylvania, the ambitious Prince initiated an aggressive policy towards his neighbours, Wallachia and Moldavia. He behaved like a despot, ignoring the wishes of the Diet, and antagonised the population of the country, especially the citizens of the Saxon towns, with

---

31 Katalin Péter, 'The Golden Age of the Principality (1606–1660)', in László Makkai, Zoltán Szász (eds), History of Transylvania, vol. II (New York. Columbia University Press, 2002), pp.5–7.

32 Zsolt Trócsányi, 'Rákóczi Zsigmond (Egy dinasztia születése)', A Debreceni Déri Múzeum Évkönyve 1978 (1979), pp.57–111.

33 László Makkai, 'István Bocskai's Insurrectionary Army', Béla K. Király, János M. Bak (eds), From Hunyadi to Rakoczi. War and Society in Late Medieval and Early Modern Hungary (New York: Columbia University Press, 1982), p.293.

his excessive demands. A strong opposition gradually developed among the political elite of the country. In March 1610, the Prince barely escaped an assassination attempt orchestrated by members of the Kendi and Kornis families. Later that year, in December, he entered the town of Sibiu with a large retinue of soldiers. Since this was one of the richest and best fortified towns in Transylvania, Gabriel Báthory declared it his new princely seat, ignoring thus the privileges of the Saxon community. Through force and intimidation he subdued the citizens of Sibiu who would never forget, nor forgive this transgression.[34] Although it was a cold winter and snow was blocking the mountain passes, Báthory marched his troops into Wallachia. Radu Șerban decided to avoid a confrontation with his troublesome neighbour and left the country. The Prince was unable to efficiently control his hajdú troops, who decided to return to their settlements on the western frontier, plundering the countryside on their way. The reputation of the prince was further diminished by their unruly behaviour.

Meanwhile, the Saxons requested the aid of Radu Șerban, who had returned to Wallachia after Báthory withdrew most of his troops across the Carpathians. The Wallachian ruler had excellent relations with the Saxon merchants and had a personal grudge against the Transylvanian Prince. Radu Șerban and his troops crossed the Transylvanian border and defeated Báthory near Brașov, on 8 July 1611.[35] Báthory was able to escape during the battle and retreated to Sibiu. Here he was besieged by Serban's troops while a new enemy, Zsigmond Forgách, approached with an army from Upper Hungary. All the odds were stacked up against Báthory but Turkish intervention, led by Omer Pasha of Bosnia, forced the two besieging armies to retreat.

The Transylvanian Prince was unable to fully restore his authority in the following year. The most notable rebels were gathered around the Saxon judge, Michael Weiss, in the town of Brașov. Aware of his despotic tendencies as ruler, the Turks were no longer willing to help him maintain order in Transylvania. On 15 October 1612, Báthory managed to defeat the rebel army gathered around Michael Weiss, who lost his life on the battlefield. He also began negotiations with the Habsburgs opting for their help to maintain his throne against the wish of the Sultan. In the meantime, Gabriel Bethlen, who had been one of his chief advisors, managed to convince the Turks that he was a better choice to rule Transylvania. In March 1613 the Sultan acknowledged his claim and offered military support for this endeavour. In October, Bethlen entered Transylvania escorted by a very large army of Turks, Tatars and Wallachians, allegedly 80,000 soldiers. The Diet was summoned on 23 October 1613 and elected the new Prince, fearing the repercussions of disobeying the Sublime Porte. Báthory, who had retreated to the western

34 Georg Kraus, *Cronica Transilvaniei 1608–1665*, eds G. Duzinchevici, E. Reus-Mîrza (București: Editura Academiei Republicii Populare Române, 1965), pp.7–9.

35 Constantin Rezachevici, 'Viața politică în primele trei decenii ale secolului al XVII–lea. Epoca lui Radu Șerban, a Movileștilorși a lui Gabriel Bethlen', Virgil Cândea (ed.), *Istoria Românilor*, vol. V (București: Editura Enciclopedică, 2003), p.51.

Gabriel Báthory, Prince of
Transylvania 1608–1613,
*Trachten-Kabinett von
Siebenbürgens*, 1729.
(The National Museum of
Transylvanian History, Cluj-
Napoca, Romania)

frontier, to Oradea, was murdered four days later by some of his own soldiers.[36]

Thus, a princely assassination and the massive presence of foreign troops ended the first phase in the history of the Transylvanian Principality. For more than seven decades, the new state struggled to survive in a region that was disputed by two powerful empires. Gradually, the rulers of Transylvania claimed the title of prince. They were elected by the representatives of the political estates of the country and acknowledged by their suzerain, the Ottoman sultan. However not all Transylvanian rulers proved to be obedient vassals. The second half of the sixteenth century and the beginning of the seventeenth century was a period of social and institutional transformation for Transylvania. Over these troubled decades, the political, administrative, social and military structures of the new state were redefined and consolidated.

The Authority of the Transylvanian Prince

Although John Sigismund Szapolyai inherited his throne, the Transylvanian estates gradually imposed their right to elect the ruler. The free election was followed, in theory, by the recognition of the suzerain power, the Sublime Porte. This was no mere formality because usually the estates were careful to choose someone who was accepted by the Porte, and in some cases Ottoman approval preceded the actual election, as happened in 1613. The power of a ruler in an elective monarchy was limited by certain conditions imposed upon him at the time of the election. Those who elected him, the representatives of the estates, aimed to ensure their political survival and to prioritise the 'common good' in the act of governance.[37] In the case of Transylvania, these terms of election were not necessarily seen as limitations of princely authority, but rather as general guidelines for internal and external policy. As a vassal of the Ottoman Empire, the prince had to pay a yearly tribute as a sign of obedience. Another important obligation was to send troops when the sultan requested them, especially during military campaigns organised on the European frontier of the Empire.[38] This was the 'constitutional framework' on which the authority of the prince was built but,

---

36 Péter, '*The Golden Age*', pp.35–36.
37 Roşu, *Elective Monarchy*, pp.194–195.
38 Tasin Gemil, *Romanians and Ottomans in the XIVth–XVIth centuries* (Bucureşti: Editura Enciclopedică, 2009), pp.61–62.

as we have seen in the earlier, many Transylvanian rulers eluded the will of the estates and made decisions against the political interest of the Porte.

One of the most important princely prerogatives was summoning the Diets (estates assemblies). The prince decided on the date and place of the meeting. He also took part in all the sessions of the Diet and enforced the laws and decisions established on these occasions. Negotiating and signing treaties with foreign countries was another important aspect of princely authority. Although this prerogative was limited by Ottoman suzerainty the Transylvanian rulers often took independent initiatives in their external policy, sometimes contrary to the interest of the Ottomans. The estates also tried to limit the authority of the prince in matters of foreign policy by imposing specific limitations during the election process. The obligation to keep the peace, to respect Ottoman suzerainty or to maintain good relations with Wallachia and Moldavia were among the most common conditions imposed by the estates in this regard. The prince had the right to send envoys and diplomats. He signed their letters of safe conduct and their credentials. On most occasions he personally received foreign envoys.

The prince had an important role in financial decision making. He presented motions regarding the level of taxes during Diets. He also administered other sources of revenues like the princely estates, mines, rents, trade monopolies and customs. He also had the right to exempt from taxes, individuals or entire communities, for various reasons like natural calamities or faithful service. The Transylvanian prince acted as supreme judge and had the right to preside over any trial. The right to award a pardon for any kind of crime was one of his most important judicial prerogatives.[39]

The Prince was the commander-in-chief of the Transylvanian army. He had the right to declare war and to conclude peace. The call to arms was made by the prince after consulting the council. He organised military inspections, musters (*lustratio*), especially before major military campaigns. He appointed superior officers, especially the Capitan General (*supremus capitaneus/capitaneus generalis*), who acted as representative of the prince (*locumtenens*) when he did not attend campaigns personally.[40]

The Diet

The Diet (*comitia/congregatio*) was a complex institution with legislative, judicial and administrative functions. It was a general assembly of the ruling prince and the representatives of the Transylvanian estates, or so-called 'political nations'. The Principality had inherited the political structure established during the Middle Ages, with three estates: the nobility, the Saxon University and the Székely. Romanians were not recognised as a distinct 'political nation', and most members of their social elite were already integrated in the nobility of the country. Besides the delegates of the estates,

---

39 Anton Dörner, 'Power Structure', in Ioan-Aurel Pop, Thomas Nägler, András Magyari (eds), *The History of Transylvania*, vol. II (Cluj-Napoca: Centre for Transylvanian Studies. Romanian Cultural Institute, 2009), pp.137–138.

40 Florin Nicolae Ardelean, 'Military Leadership in the Transylvanian Principality. The Captain General in the second half of the sixteenth century', *Banatica*, 26–2 (2016), pp.337–349.

the members of the council, important office holders, representatives of major towns and various persons who received direct invitations from the prince, attended the Diet. Usually a total of 130–150 people participated in each session. Diets were usually summoned twice a year in various locations across Transylvania, such as Turda, Cluj, Alba Iulia, Sibiu, Sighişoara, Bistriţa, Târgu Mureş, Făgăraş, etc. A session lasted between one and three weeks. Law initiatives were taken by representatives of the estates but the prince could also take such initiatives directly or indirectly through one of his noble guests. Sometimes, trials took place during Diets and, in most cases, were chaired by the prince himself.[41]

Various subjects were debated during Diet sessions. The most common were taxes, foreign policy, administrative issues and aspects of military organisation. The army represented the greatest financial burden for most early modern European states and Transylvania was no exception. Recruitment, weapon standards, organisation of musters, the military obligations of the estates, foreign mercenaries, construction and modernisation of fortifications, provisioning and garrisons, all these matters were debated by the prince and the estates during Diet sessions.[42] Religious topics were also very common, especially during the first decades of the Principality. The Reformation was very successful in Transylvania and a significant number of communities adhered to various protestant confessions that were spreading throughout Europe in the sixteenth century. In 1568, the Diet of Turda, set the principle of freedom to worship and allowed communities to choose their denomination. In spite of the apparent tolerance, further religious innovation was prohibited and in 1595 the Diet established a system of four accepted denominations (*receptae*): Catholicism, Lutheranism, Calvinism and Unitarianism. Orthodoxy was only tolerated, which meant it was not represented in the ruling circles and was dependent on the benevolence of the prince.[43]

The Council of the Prince

The Council of the Prince was another important political institution which had the role to advise the ruler in compliance with the laws of the country. The Council was first established in 1542 by Bishop Martinuzzi, who was the leading councillor of the infant John Sigismund Szapolyai at the time. All three estates, Nobles, Saxons and Székely, were represented within the council. During the following years, the Diet established the composition of the Council (*concilium intimum*) at 22 members, seven representing each nation and the Catholic bishop of Alba Iulia. The members of the Council were chosen by the Diet. From 1548 onwards representatives of the *Partium* counties were also included in this ruling institution. In 1558 the Council

---

41 Dörner, 'Power Structure', p.162.

42 Zsolt Trócsányi, *Törvényalkotás az Erdélyi Fejedelemségben* (Budapest: Gondolat, 2005), pp.134–162.

43 Edith Szegedi, 'The birth and evolution of the Principality of Transylvania', in Ioan-Aurel Pop, Thomas Nägler, András Magyari (eds), *The History of Transylvania*, vol. II (Cluj-Napoca: Centre for Transylvanian Studies. Romanian Cultural Institute, 2009), pp.104–105.

was limited to 12 persons.[44] The authority of the prince increased during the last decades of the sixteenth century and influenced the election of council members. Councillors were chosen from the loyal supporters of the rulers and were also given important administrative and military offices. The most important councillor was the chancellor.[45]

Administrative Organisation

The administrative structure of the voivodate of Transylvania was maintained during the era of the Principality. The most common administrative units were counties, seats and districts.

There were seven Transylvanian counties: Inner – Szolnok, Dăbâca, Alba, Hunedoara, Târnava, Turda and Cluj. These administrative units were led by counts (*comes, ispán*) which were named by the ruling prince. The count exercised fiscal, administrative, judicial and military authority. He was helped in his activity by a vice-count, usually a representative of the local nobility.[46] The counties, situated between the Western Carpathians and the Tisa River, which came under the authority of Transylvanian rulers during the second half of the sixteenth century, were Maramureş, Szabolcs, Satu-Mare, Middle – Szolnok, Bihor, Outer – Szolnok, Békés, Csongrád, Arad, Cenad, and Timiş. In time, some of these territories were lost to the Habsburgs or to the Ottomans.[47] The counties were inhabited by nobles and their serfs.

The term 'seat' as an administrative unit derives from the territorial legal courts named 'seats of judgment' (*sedes judiciaria*). The Transylvanian Saxons, descendants of German and other Western European settlers, were organised in nine seats, situated in the southern and eastern parts of Transylvania: Orăştie, Sebeş, Miercurea, Sibiu, Nocrich, Cincu, Sighişoara, Rupea, Mediaş and Şeica. In 1552 Şeica was unified with the seat of Mediaş. Two districts were organised around the towns of Braşov and Bistriţa. Each Saxon seat was ruled by a judge (*iudex regius*) who had similar prerogatives as the counts. All these administrative units were part of the so-called *Universitas Saxonum*, and all their free inhabitants represented one of the Transylvanian estates.[48] In terms of political orientation, the Saxons were usually supporters of the Habsburgs. This attitude was determined by their connections with merchant families in the German Empire and German families in the towns of Royal Hungary, ruled by Habsburg kings. They were also the most ardent promoters of the Reformation in Transylvania. The most remarkable personality involved in this process was Johannes Honterus. On

---

44 Dörner, 'Power Structure', pp.151–152.
45 Teréz Oborni, 'State and governance in the Principality of Transylvania', *Hungarian Studies*, 27:2 (2013), p.321.
46 Dörner, 'Power Structure', pp.173–174.
47 Makkai, 'The first period of the Principality', p.616.
48 Dörner, 'Power Structure', pp.175–176.

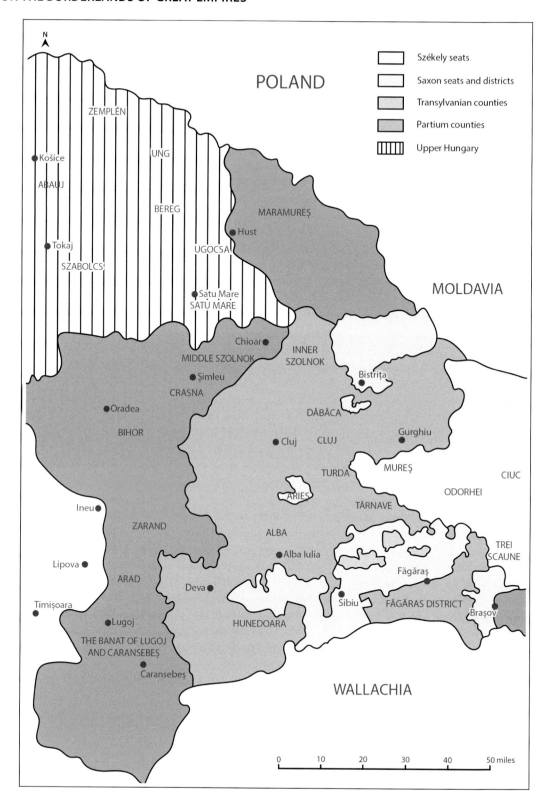

Transylvania after the Peace Treaty of Speyer (1570).

28 November 1545, a general assembly of the Universitas Saxonum ruled that the Lutheran creed must be generally adopted in their territories.[49]

The Székely community constituted the third estate in the Principality of Transylvania and inhabited the border region in the south-eastern parts of the country. They received these territories from Hungarian kings in the early phase of the conquest of Transylvania. They had a very particular social status. They were neither true nobles nor serfs, because they enjoyed collective privileges and tax exemptions based on their obligation to perform military duty. In time their defensive role was diminished and Székely society suffered radical transformations during the age of the Principality. The poorer members of the community willingly gave up their freedom and became serfs while the elite tended to become part of the true nobility, through service at the princely court and by acquiring estates outside the Székely seats. In 1562 this community was organised in five administrative seats: Odorhei, Trei Scaune, Mureş, Arieş and Ciuc. The most important office in a Székely seat was that of captain (*capitaneus sedis siculicalis*).[50]

The territories which were under the direct control of the prince, the so-called fiscal estate, had a distinct administrative status. Most of these estates were concentrated around important fortifications, especially on the border of the Principality. By the end of the sixteenth century the fiscal estate included about 700 villages, representing almost 20 percent of the Transylvanian territory. The most important domains were Alba Iulia, Deva, Oradea, Făgăraş, Chioar, Gurghiu, Cluj-Mănăştur, Gherla, Ineu, Lugoj, Caransebeş, Odorheiul Secuiesc, Leţ, Zlatna and Hust.[51]

Romanians and Other Ethnic Communities

The ethnic composition of Transylvania was and still is very complex. The medieval and early modern estates did not overlap with any particular ethnicity, with the exception of the Székely. Saxon settlers had arrived in Transylvania from various western European regions although the German element was predominant. Most Transylvanian noble families had Hungarian origins, but they also included a significant number of Romanian, Croatian and Serbian families.

Romanians were present in most Transylvanian villages, but they were more concentrated in certain regions like Haţeg district, Făgăraş district, Maramureş County and the mountainous regions of Bihor, Arad, Zarand and Banat. Sheep husbandry was a specific occupation of Romanians. There were several Transylvanian noble families who had Romanian origins, but they had been integrated, both legally and culturally, into the noble estate. The remaining Romanian social elite, *cnezi, juzi* and *crainici*, were not recognised

---

49 István Keul, *Early Modern Religious Communities in East-Central Europe: Ethnic Diversity, Denominational Plurality and Corporative Politics in the Principality of Transylvania (1526–1691)* (Leiden, Boston: Brill, 2009), p.258.
50 Dörner, 'Power Structure', pp.177–178.
51 Makkai, 'The first period of the Principality', p.727.

as true nobles although they kept some prerogatives and military obligations typical for their noble status.[52]

From a cultural and confessional point of view, Romanians in Transylvania were part of the Eastern, Orthodox world. There were some initiatives to convert Romanians to the new Protestant denominations, but they enjoyed limited success. To counter the effect of Reformation in his country, the Catholic prince Stephen Báthory supported the organisation of a higher hierarchy of the Orthodox Church in Transylvania.[53]

Migration was an intense process that constantly diversified the ethnic composition of the region. Several communities of foreign origin were already established in Transylvania before the Principality was organised and other groups came during the sixteenth and the seventeenth centuries. Roma (Gypsies), Jewish, Polish, Czech, Slovak, Greek and Armenian communities were among the best represented. South Slavic populations, especially Serbs and Croats, had also moved to Transylvania as the Ottoman conquest advanced in the Balkan Peninsula. Noble families but also larger groups settled mostly in the Banat area and along the Mureş valley.[54]

Nobility and Other Privileged Social Categories

Nobility constituted the political and economic elite of society. In the Transylvanian Principality those who enjoyed noble status were rather numerous in comparison to other parts of Europe. According to a rough estimation they represented about 12 percent of the whole population. Nobility was inherited and could be given to any individual by the ruling prince for extraordinary merits. Land ownership was not a necessary condition as there were nobles with land possessions (*possessionati*) or those who lacked such proprieties (*impossessionati*). Most political, administrative and military offices were held by nobles, while the Székely and the Saxons had limited access to such positions. Noble status was guaranteed by performing military duty. That is why, even during the early modern period, the bulk of the Transylvanian army was composed of nobles and other groups who enjoyed a privileged status.[55] It was a medieval feature of the Transylvanian military organization that didn't obstruct the evolution of paid military

---

52 Florin Nicolae Ardelean, *Organizarea militară în principatul Transilvaniei (1541–1691): Comitate şi domenii fiscale* (Cluj-Napoca: Academia Română. Centrul de Studii Transilvane, 2019), pp.235–241.

53 Ovidiu Ghitta, 'Biserica Ortodoxă din Transilvania', in Ioan-Aurel Pop, Thomas Nägler, András Magyari (eds), *Istoria Transilvaniei*, vol. II (Cluj-Napoca: Institutul Cultural Român. Centrul de Studii Transilvane, 2005), pp.263–270.

54 Nenad Lemajić, 'The Serbian Population of the Banat and the Western Mureş Basin in the fifteenth and sixteenth Centuries (and its Local and Military Leaders)', in Đura Hardi (ed.), *The Cultural and Historical Heritage of Vojvodina in the Context of Classical and Medieval Studies* (Novi Sad: Faculty of Philosophy, 2015), pp.205–223; Adrian Magina, 'Le long voyage vers la terre promise: Les migrations serbes en banat (XVe–XVIe siècles)', in Florin Nicolae Ardelean, Cristopher Nicholson, Johannes Preiser-Kapeller (eds), *Between Worlds: The Age of the Jagiellonians* (Frankfurt am Main: Peter Lang Edition, 2013), pp.129–140.

55 Ardelean, *Organizarea militară*, pp.51–83.

service as we shall see in the following chapters.

Several other groups, within the Transylvanian social framework, benefited from a limited privileged status. In other words they were not members of the 'true nobility' (*una eademque nobilitas*) but they were neither peasants. The *hajdús* performed military duties in the frontier area. They were established within the borders of the Principality (mainly in Bihor County) or in Royal Hungary. They gained collective privileges during the anti-Habsburg rebellion of Stephen Bocskai, 1604–1606. The boyars from Făgăraş formed a particular group of Romanian nobles in southern Transylvania. They performed military service like the other nobles of the country, but their privileges were recognised only inside their designated administrative unit, Făgăraş district. There were other similar groups who were exempted from paying taxes in exchange for military duties. Known under various names: soldiers (*puskások*, *pixidari*), guardsmen (*darabontok*) and freemen (*libertines*), they formed semi-permanent military forces established on the estates of the main Transylvanian fortifications.[56]

Townsfolk

In early modern Transylvania, the inhabitants of urban settlements represented less than five percent of the population. The most developed towns were located in the seats and districts of the Saxons and were important centres of commerce and crafts. The patricians constituted an urban social and economic elite, and they held all the ruling positions within the political hierarchy of every town.[57]

The most developed urban settlement outside the Saxon lands was Cluj, with a population of about 8,000 inhabitants, almost as large as Braşov (about 9,000 inhabitants), the largest Saxon settlement. Cluj developed during this difficult period because it had a better strategic position on the trade route that linked Transylvania to Upper Hungary and central Europe.

Market towns (*mezőváros, oppidum*) were increasing in size and number especially in the Hungarian plain during the latter Middle Ages. Their economic activity was centred on the trade of agricultural products and cattle. From a juridical point of view the inhabitants of these settlements were serfs, living on noble or royal estates. However they were able to redeem their work obligations with money. Crafts were also developing as secondary economic activities. The largest market town under Transylvanian authority was Debrecen, in Bihor County. Its development was affected by military activity and by the peculiar situation of paying taxes to more than one authority. Debrecen was officially part of the Principality of Transylvania, but it lay at the junction of three state borders, and thus, from 1567 onwards, it had to pay an annual tax to Transylvania (3,200 florins), the Ottoman Empire (2,000 florins) and

---

56 Ionuţ Costea, 'Social structures', in Ioan-Aurel Pop, Thomas Nägler, András Magyari (eds), *The History of Transylvania*, vol. II (Cluj-Napoca: Center for Transylvanian Studies. Romanian Cultural Institute, 2009), pp.208–221.

57 Costea, 'Social structures', p.231.

Royal Hungary (1,000 florins). In spite of these unfavourable developments, Debrecen remained the largest and most prosperous urban settlement under the authority of the Transylvanian rulers. In the middle of the sixteenth century this town had about 1,300 tax-paying households, indicating a population of about 20,000 inhabitants.[58]

Peasants

Villains (*iobagiones, colones*), dependent peasants, formed the most numerous social class in the Transylvanian Principality. They lived on fiscal, noble or ecclesiastical lands and were the main workforce involved in agriculture. They paid taxes to both their landlords and the country, and, within certain limits, they were also drafted for military service. The amount of taxes (in money or produce) as well as work obligations (*gratuitis labor*) was established by each landowner independently, although there were some initiatives to impose certain standards in this regard. Landless peasants, cotters (*inquilini*), gained their existence by working as day labourers or by performing various crafts. They enjoyed freedom of movement and were a free social group from a juridical point of view. It is estimated that they represented less than 10 percent of the non-privileged population of the country.[59]

58　Makkai, 'The first period of the Principality', pp.680–681.
59　Costea, 'Social structures', pp.231–232.

2

The Organisation of the Transylvanian Army

The Transylvanian army was a 'mirror reflection' of the community it was meant to protect. The complex structure of society, with its various groups and categories, each with its own privileges, freedoms and obligations are represented within the military organisation. Between 1541 and 1613 the armed forces of the Transylvanian rulers were in a process of transition. Medieval tradition was intertwined with early modern innovation. Military service was mostly based on privilege and tax exemption, but mercenaries (soldiers who received regular wages) became more and more common in time. The prince was the supreme commander but in order to mobilise certain elements of the army he needed the consent of the Diet. The military prerogatives of the prince were in theory limited by other institutions, but also by the impact of suzerainty with the Ottoman Empire.

Nobility

In the Kingdom of Hungary, like all over medieval Europe, nobles fulfilled the role of warriors (*bellatores*). During the fourteenth and the fifteenth centuries two different noble military structures developed in the Realm of Saint Stephen, the baronial *banderia* and the noble levy.

The upper echelons of the Hungarian nobility, the so-called barons (*barones*), were able to recruit large military contingents from their vast estates. These private baronial armies thrived during the interregnum marked by the end of the Arpadian dynasty (1290) and the arrival of the first Angevin king, Charles Robert (1308).[1] The baronial armies were referred to as 'banners' (*vexilium, banderia*) because they bore the coat of arms of the baron they represented. The Italian term *banderia* was most commonly used

---

1   János M. Bak, 'Politics, Society and Defence in Medieval and Early Modern Hungary', in Béla K. Király, János M. Bak (eds), *From Hunyadi to Rákoczi: War and Society in Late Medieval and Early Modern Hungary* (New York: Columbia University Press, 1982), p.7.

in contemporary sources, starting with the fourteenth century.[2] A *banderia* was composed of lesser nobles (*servientes, familiares*) who chose to enter the service of a baron. The *familiares* performed mostly military service but occasionally they were entrusted with other administrative or economic tasks. In exchange for their service they were rewarded with wages, propriety or access to lesser positions in the administrative apparatus of the kingdom.[3] In the fourteenth century several Hungarian barons were able to recruit large contingents of more than one thousand fighting men. The basic military unit was the lance, consisting of one heavily armoured horsemen accompanied by two or three light riders (*pharetrarii*).[4] During the reigns of the Jagiellonian kings, Wladislas II (1490–1516) and Louis II (1516–1526), the military role of the barons was greatly increased. The reforms of Wladislas II created a decentralised military system which relied on the military contingents of the major landowners and office holders of the kingdom. Due to intensified confrontations with the Ottomans, the number of light cavalry, hussars (*levis armature vulgo Huszarones nuncupati*), was greater than that of heavy cavalry (*armigeri*).[5]

The noble levy consisted of the middle and lower ranks of the county nobility, who were not serving in a baronial *banderia*. According to the Golden Bull of King Andrew II, issued in 1222, every noble of the kingdom had the obligation to join the army (*exercitus generalis*). The royal counts were entrusted with the mobilisation and leadership of the troops recruited in their county. The noble insurrection was proclaimed only when the country was menaced by an external threat.[6] In theory all nobles were expected to fight mounted with heavy defensive armour, but most of those who joined the levy were unable to procure such expensive equipment.[7] Although their fighting value was questionable, the *exercitus generalis* was able to muster a significant number of soldiers. During the decades that preceded to the battle of Mohács (1526), the effectives of this military structure are estimated at 18,500–22,500 soldiers.[8]

The privileges and obligations of the nobility were maintained although Transylvania was making a transition from being a province within a larger kingdom to becoming a distinct state. No noble family from this region

---

2   Pál Engel, *Regatul Sfântului Ştefan: Istoria Ungariei medievale 895–1526* (Cluj-Napoca: Editura Mega, 2006), p.211.

3   Martyn Rady, *Nobility, Land and Service in Medieval Hungary* (Basingstoke: Palgrave, 2000), p.147.

4   Attila Barany, 'King Sigismund of Luxemburg and the preparations for the Hungarian crusading host of Nicopolis (1386–396)', in Daniel Baloup, Manuel Sánchez Martínez (eds), *Partir en croisade à la fin de Moyen Âge. Financement et logistique* (Toulouse: Presses universitaires du Midi, 2015), p.159.

5   Tamás Pálosfalvi, *From Nicopolis to Mohács: a history of Ottoman–Hungarian warfare, 1389–1526* (Leiden; Boston: Brill, 2018), pp.41–43.

6   *Corpus Juris Hungarici seu Decretum Generale Inclyti Regni Hungariae Partiumque eidem Annexarum* (Budae, 1822), Decretum Anii 1222, art. 7, p.151.

7   Joseph Held, 'Military Reform in Early Fifteenth Century Hungary', *East European Quarterly*, XI: 2 (1977), p.132.

8   András Kubinyi, 'Hungary's Power Factions and the Turkish Threat in the Jagiellonian Period (1490–1526)', in István Zombori (ed.), *Fight against the Turk in Central-Europe in the first half of the 16th century* (Budapest, 2004), p.129.

had the economic means of maintaining a *banderia*, thus the main military structure that survived was the noble levy. In addition, there were attempts to organise permanent military contingents representing the three estates of the country, including the nobility.

The coexistence of these two military structures was established early on. At the Diet of Sighișoara, on 29 August 1540, the nobility agreed to pay a tax of 50 denars for each *porta* (fiscal unit) for military purposes. The money gathered this way was meant to sustain a contingent of 1,000 cavalry who would be constantly in the service of the two captain generals, Stephen Mailat and Imrè Balassa. The Saxons and the Székelys had similar obligations, each providing 1,000 soldiers. In addition, if the country was threatened by a large military force, the whole country was expected to mobilise (*totum regnum insurgat*).[9]

In the following years the Diet established further details regarding the military obligations of the nobility. All those who joined the army were expected to bring their own food supplies and if necessary, they could buy from local merchants at pre-established prices. According to the provisions of the Diet of Turda, from March 1542, nobles were expected to fight on horseback, but exceptions were acknowledged. A warhorse, lance, shield, helmet and breastplate (*habeat equum, arma, hastam, clypeum, galeam, et loricam*) were mandatory for all those who could afford such equipment. Poor nobles could perform their military duties as infantry armed with firearms (*habeat saltem pixidem*).[10] The permanent cavalry detachment of the nobility was periodically mentioned during estates assemblies. The conditions of recruitment were the same, only the number of soldiers varied from one session to another: 500 in February 1543,[11] 1,000 in November 1543,[12] and 2,000 in 1548 and 1549.[13]

On some occasions, the nobility of certain counties mobilised and performed small scale military actions within the boundaries of their administrative units. In 1550, a small Turkish army led by Kasim Pasha marched through the territories of Hunedoara County. The local count (*ispán*), János Török, gathered his soldiers and confronted the Turks in the vicinity of the Deva fortress. His small army consisted of 113 cavalry and 673 infantry. The young Transylvanian count was driven by the desire of revenge because his father, Bálint Török, was imprisoned by the Ottomans and held in the Yedikule. During the battle, Török duelled and defeated a Turkish officer, Feru Aga.[14] Such duels were quite common and were a distinctive feature of early modern warfare on the European border of the Ottoman Empire.

Although they brought a consistent detachment of foreign mercenaries with them in 1551, the Habsburgs adhered to the specific Transylvanian

---

9   *MCRT*, vol. I, pp.40–41.
10   *MCRT*, vol. I, p.171
11   *MCRT*, vol. I, p.177.
12   *MCRT*, vol. I, p.183.
13   *MCRT*, vol. I, pp.239, 298.
14   Magyar Tudományos Akadémia Könyvtára, Kézirattár, Budapest, Ms. 4178/3, Endre Veress, *Arcélek Erdély viharos multjából, Castaldo tábornok Erdélyben (1551–1553)*, f. 48.

military system. The military potential of the local nobility was acknowledged by the new masters of Transylvania. The noble levy was regularly discussed during Diet sessions. In 1552, a special provision regarding weapons and equipment was voted. Nobles who joined the army were expected to have a helmet, shield, lance, breastplate and a good warhorse (*armis bellicis bene instructe, galeis scilicet clipeis ac hastis, loricis, et equis bonis quo meliori modo potuerint parate esse debeant et teneantur*).[15] Some Transylvanian nobles, who proved to be particularly loyal to the Habsburg cause, received regular wages for larger military retinues. Such was the case of András Báthory of Șimleu who entered the service of the Habsburgs with 100 horsemen.[16]

In 1556 the Habsburgs lost control over Transylvania and John Sigismund Szapolyai and his mother Isabella returned from exile. In the following decades the Transylvanian army was engaged in a protracted war against the Habsburgs on the western border of the principality and in Upper Hungary. The nobility continued to play an important role in the Transylvanian army together with the other estates. The general insurrection of the nobility was considered a slow and cumbersome process. Many nobles were unable to meet the minimal standards regarding weapons and equipment. In this context, the prince and the Diet decided that it was far more efficient to maintain a smaller permanent detachment of nobles, ranging between 500 and 2,000 horsemen. The other estates, the Saxons and the Székely, had similar obligations. Thus, the prince knew he could rely on a small but efficient army of 1,500–6,000 seasoned soldiers, able to mobilise swiftly.[17]

Stephen Báthory, the first elected Transylvanian ruler, maintained both the general insurrection and the smaller, semi-permanent detachments. During certain Diet sessions the military obligations of the nobility were debated, and new aspects were established. For example, in 1575, the Prince and the Diet agreed that nobles, who were in service at court, or in the service of other nobles, were exempted from personally attending the army. Instead they had to provide a mercenary horseman. Lesser nobles who shared the same household (members of the same family) had to provide a single armed horseman. It was also required that all those who joined the banners of counties, nobles and commoners, should wear green clothes.[18]

During the 'Long Turkish War' (1591–1606) most exemptions from military duty were annulled. In 1598, Prince Sigismund Báthory called all his nobles together in camp. They were given only nine days to arrive after they received the order of mobilisation. Those who failed to obey the summons were punished with a fine of 100 florins. For the same offence, lesser nobles had to pay a smaller fine of 12 florins.[19] The nobility played a major role in most battles and campaigns of the Long Turkish War by providing a significant proportion of the cavalry within the Transylvanian army. In the

---

15 *MCRT*, vol. I, p.405.
16 ÖStA, HHStA, Hungarica AA, Fas. 59, Konv. A, Fas. 62, Konv. A. ff. 85, 88–89; Ardelean, 'Foreign Mercenaries', p.120.
17 Ardelean, *Organizarea militară*, pp.60–64.
18 *MCRT*, vol. II, p.559.
19 *MCRT*, vol. IV, p.191.

battle of Mezőkeresztes (1596), the Transylvanian Prince joined the Habsburg forces with a small army of 8,000 soldiers, most of them cavalry.[20] Chancellor Josika István led and army of 20,000 cavalry and 8,000 infantry at the second siege of Timişoara, in 1597.[21] In the battle of Şelimbăr (28 October 1599), the army of Andrew Báthory had about 2,600 noble cavalry. This number was below the normal effective numbers of the county banners, because several Transylvanian nobles had joined the army of Michael the Brave.[22]

The nobles were sometimes reluctant to fight beyond the borders of the country. However, most Transylvanian rulers were able to overcome this issue and convinced the nobility to take part in military campaigns outside the borders of the principality. The Diet of Sebeş, 23–30 April 1611, specifically mentions the obligation of the nobility to follow the Prince (Gabriel Báthory) and to fight wherever he considered necessary. Nobles had the obligation to join the banner of the county where their main residence was located. Poor nobles, and those suffering from sickness or infirmity, were exempted from personally attending the army but had to provide a mercenary horseman for every four land plots (porta) they possessed. The same rule applied to noble widows.[23]

Interesting details about the military equipment of Transylvanian nobles are provided by foreign travellers. Giovanandrea Gromo, an Italian who served at the court of John Sigismund Szapolyai, noted that most nobles went to war on horseback. They were armed with Turkish scimitars, shields, heavy long swords, small wheel lock arquebuses and chain mail.[24] The similarity between Transylvanian and Turkish cavalry was observed by other contemporary authors. Ascanio Centorio degli Hortensii, who described the campaigns of Castaldo in Transylvania and Hungary, noted that the hussars were very similar to Ottoman cavalry. Their most common weapons were shields (targhe), Turkish lances, maces, sabres and sallet helmets (celate).[25] A similar description was provided by Anton Verancsics who claimed that Transylvanian nobles used to equip themselves as heavy cavalry (cataphracti) but in the sixteenth century most of them opted for lighter equipment, becoming hussars (velites). They were armed with a steel helmet, a chain mail (lorica hamata), a Turkish-style sabre, a large shield on their left arm, an iron glove on their right hand and a lance. Turkish horses were favoured because of their speed and mobility.[26] Transylvanian nobles used a large variety of close combat weapons like sabres, maces and scimitars, but also a particular type of long sword called the hegyestőr.[27] Such weapons were prized possessions and were sometimes recorded in the wills of high-ranking noblemen. A decorated long sword

20 Gróf Illésházy István nádor Földjegyzései 1592–1603, Gábor Kazinczy (ed.), Monumenta Hungariae Historica, Scriptores, VII (Pest, 1863), p.33; Komáromy, A Mezőkeresztesi csata, pp.281–284.

21 Gróf Illésházy István, p.51.

22 Ardelean, Organizarea militară, pp.67–68.

23 MCRT, vol. VI, pp.205–206.

24 Călători străini despre Ţările Române, vol. II, Maria Holban, Maria Matilda Alexandrescu-Dresca Bulgaru, Paul Cernovodeanu (eds), (Bucureşti: Editura Ştiinţifică şi Enciclopedică, 1973), p.321.

25 Centorio, Comentarii, p.66.

26 Călători străini, vol. I, p.416.

27 Tibor S. Kovács, Huszár-fegyverek a 15–17. Században (Budapest: Martin Opitz Kiadó, 2010), pp.128–149.

(*hegyestewr*) was among the precious items listed in the last will and testament of Leonard Barlabási of Idrifia, former vice-voivode of Transylvania, in the first half of the sixteenth century.[28]

In the autumn of 1595, the army of Prince Sigismund Báthory completed a successful campaign in Wallachia. Gyerőfi János was among the nobles who answered the summons of the Transylvanian ruler. After the conquest of Târgoviște he fell ill and wrote a letter to his wife asking for provisions and a few servants to assist him for the rest of the campaign. His plate armour and a chainmail were among the requested items. A carriage with food provisions, several wolf and fox furs, his cook and an armed servant are also mentioned in his letter.[29]

Sources from the second half of the sixteenth century use the terms hussars or lancers (*kopjások*) when referring to local cavalry. The lance (*kopja*) was the most common offensive cavalry weapon.[30] Although there are many references on the continued use of breastplates and even chainmail, the term *armiger*, which was used in previous periods to designate heavy cavalry, is very rare. Most Transylvanian nobles had limited resources and were unable to procure expensive defensive equipment. The Ottoman wars had also influenced the evolution of cavalry warfare in Hungary and Transylvania.[31] Hussars, with their lighter equipment, were better adapted to confrontations with the Turks and to the specifics of irregular warfare which dominated military conflicts in these parts of Europe.

County Militia

In the medieval kingdom of Hungary, peasants were sometimes conscripted for military service. The process of recruitment was based on the fiscal system that divided the proprieties of the nobility into land plots or peasant households (*porta*). The organisation of the first peasant militia (*militia portalis, telekkatonság*) dates from the time of Sigismund of Luxemburg (1387–1437). In 1397, at the Diet of Timișoara, it was established that each nobleman had the obligation to provide one mounted archer (*pharetrarius*) for every 20 serfs that lived on his lands.[32] The new form of recruitment was motivated by the increased Ottoman threat. In the following decades several royal decrees dealt with the organisation of the so-called 'portal militia'. The most common issues

---

28 Mária Lupescu Makó, *Talem fecisset testamentum...Testamente nobiliare din Transilvania medievală* (Cluj-Napoca: Argonaut, 2011), p.234.

29 Veress (ed.), *Documente*, vol. IV, pp.296–297.

30 János Kalmár, *Régi magyar fegyverek* (Budapest: Natura, 1971), pp.41–43.

31 János B. Szabó, Győző Somogy, *Az Erdélyi fejedelemség hadserege* (Budapest: Zrinyi Kiadó, 1996), p.16; János B. Szabó, 'The Army of the Szapolyai Family during the Reign of John Szapolyai and John Sigismund (Baronial, Voivodal and Royal Troops, 1510–1571)', Pál Fodor and Szabolcs Varga (eds), *A Forgotten Hungarian Royal Dynasty: The Szapolyais* (Budapest: Research Center for Humanities, 2020), p.224.

32 András Borosy, 'The Militia Portalis in Hungary before 1526', in János M. Bak, Béla K. Király (eds), *From Hunyadi to Rakoczi. War and Society in Late Medieval and Early Modern Hungary* (New York: Columbia University Press, 1982), p.63.

were the rate of conscription and weapon standards. According to the earliest decrees (1397, 1433, 1435) the militia consisted of mounted archers. In 1454 the sources mention infantry armed with spears and shields, heavy cavalry in 1459 (most probably mercenaries paid through contributions that replaced direct recruitment), or light cavalry (hussars) and infantry armed with firearms in 1518.[33] Sometimes the direct recruitment of peasants was replaced with a tax. When peasants did join the royal army, they were exempted from paying the census tax, as in 1459.[34] The presence of peasant soldiers on the battlefield has been questioned by some historians and besides the central legislation of the Hungarian kingdom there is little evidence on how this system of recruitment actually worked. An important exception would be the report of Pasquale da Sorgo on the second battle of Kosovo (1448), which mentions a detachment of 8,000 cavalry provided by the people of Hungary on the basis of one horseman for every 50 land plots.[35]

The recruitment of peasants for military duty was maintained in the Transylvanian Principality. According to the decisions of the Diet of Turda, from December 1542 the militias of the counties would be called to arms only if the contingents provided by the nobility and the other estates (Saxons and Székely) were insufficient in number. The rate of conscription in the counties was established at one horseman for every 10 peasant households (*porta*).[36] In 1551 the peasant militia was conceived as a partial mobilisation of serfs living on the lands of the nobility. In cases where it was necessity, one out of every 16 serfs was recruited (*sedecima parte colonorum levata*).[37]

Most data on the organisation of peasant militias is provided by central legislation (the decisions of the Diets). However there are other sources which confirm the fact that the militia was actually mobilised and took part in major military action. General Castaldo refers to conscripted peasants in some of his reports sent to the Habsburg Emperor.[38] In 1551, during the siege of Lipova, 7,000 soldiers from the Transylvanian army represented the nobility (the noble insurrection) and the peasants recruited from their estates.[39] The military conscription of peasants from Bihor county in 1551 is confirmed by a letter of Bishop Martinuzzi, which mentions the fact that those who were taken into the army were exempted from working on the construction of Szolnok fortress.[40]

A more detailed regulation regarding the peasant militia was issued in 1557, while the Transylvanian army was mustering near Cluj. The nobility

---

33   Borosy, 'The Militia Portalis', pp.63–80; Held, 'Military Reform', pp.135–138.

34   Ferenc Döry, György Bónis (eds), *Decreta Regni Hungariae*, vol. II (Budapest: Akadémia Kiadó, 1989), p.111.

35   Mark Whelan, 'Pasquale da Sorgo and the Second Battle of Kosovo (1448): A Translation', *Slavonic and East European Review*, 94:1, 2016, pp.133–135.

36   *MCRT*, vol. I, p.171; David Prodan, *Iobăgia în Transilvania în secolul al XVI-lea*, vol. I (București, Editura Academiei, 1967), p.397.

37   *MCRT*, vol. I, p.317.

38   ÖStA, HHStA, Hungarica AA, Fas. 58, Konv. C, f. 157–159; Fas. 49, Konv. A, f. 1–3.

39   ÖStA, HHStA, Hungarica AA, Fas. 60, Konv. A, f. 91.

40   Eudoxiu de Hurmuzaki (ed.), *Documente privitoare la Istoria Românilor*, vol. II/4 (București: Academia Română și Ministerul Cultelor și Instrucțiunii Publice, 1894), p.594.

was expected to arrive with small contingents of peasants from their estates, one soldier for every 16 serfs (*cum sedecima parte colonorum suorum iuxta connumeracionem*). Every 20 peasant soldiers had to bring a carriage with provisions. Those who joined the army were entitled to regular wages for the duration of the campaign. They were given eight days to arrive in camp and were expected to be armed with firearms or with bows and spears (*quibus se poterunt pixidibus, alij cum arcubus, reliqui cum lanceis, iuxta antiquam eorum consuetudinem, huc veniat ad 8 diem cum bellico apparatu*).[41]

The size of county militias can be deduced by analysing fiscal conscription records, since there are no direct sources to shed light on this particular matter. The number of recruited soldiers depended on the conscription rate and the number of registered households in each administrative unit. During the second half of the sixteenth century, Bihor – the largest county under the authority of Transylvanian rulers – should have been able to muster about 657 soldiers at a conscription rate of one soldier for every 10 households. Smaller counties had smaller militias; Middle Szolnok: 129 soldiers, Crasna: 82 and Maramureș: 60.[42]

Sometimes, at the end of a military campaign, peasants refused to return to their homes and wandered the countryside organised in small bands. This problem was acknowledged by Transylvanian authorities and in 1566 the Diet issued an edict which established harsh punishment for such vagabonds. At the same time each noble was held responsible for disarming the peasants recruited from his estates at the end of the expedition.[43]

Stephen Báthory was the first Transylvanian ruler who organised regular musters for the county militias. The rate of conscription was doubled, two soldiers, one horseman and one foot soldier, were recruited for every 16 serfs.[44]

During the Long Turkish War (1591–1606), the county militias were once again an important subject of debate during Diet sessions. The rate of conscription was established at one soldier for every 10 serfs. The paymaster (*fizetőmester*) became a permanent position among the officials of the Transylvanian court. His wage was 40 florins a month while the captain general was rewarded with 300 florins a month, a lieutenant (*hadnágy*) eight florins a month, a flag bearer five florins a month, a drummer four florins a month, a sergeant (*decurionus*) four florins a month, a common cavalryman three florins a month and a common infantryman two florins a month.[45]

At the end of this protracted conflict the militia was in a state of decline because the fiscal system, which was the basis for recruitment, was no longer valid. Constant warfare, radical political changes and the presence of foreign troops determined a high degree of mobility among the population of the country. The conscription registers compiled in previous years were no longer useful because many villages were burned down, Tatars had taken a

---

41 *MCRT*, vol. II, pp.85–86.
42 Ardelean, *Organizarea militară*, pp.98–100.
43 *MCRT*, vol. II, p.325.
44 *MCRT*, vol. II, pp.559–560.
45 *MCRT*, vol. III, pp.440–442.

significant number of prisoners and most of the remaining villagers found refuge in forests and mountain areas.[46]

During the sixteenth century the peasant militia was conceived as an auxiliary element of the Transylvanian army. Such militias were organised mainly in the counties, but the Saxon seats also drafted commoners for military service in their militia. The mobilisation of peasant soldiers was initiated only in exceptional circumstances, and it was the easiest way of increasing the numbers of soldiers in the Transylvanian army. Exemption from taxes and wages (especially towards the end of the sixteenth century) were the main means of compensation. Military service was also the most important way for a commoner to gain noble status.

Székely

The Székely (*Siculi*) benefited from privileges and tax exemptions, as a community, in exchange for military service. In the twelfth century they fought in the vanguard of the Hungarian army as horse archers. As the Hungarian conquest of Transylvania advanced, they were settled in the south-eastern parts of the province and their main purpose was to defend the border of the kingdom in this region.[47] In the second half of the fifteenth century, Székely society underwent a process of stratification that was also reflected in their military organisation. According to an edict issued by King Matthias Corvinus, in 1473, the elite of the Székely community, *primores* (also called *primipili* or *lófők*) performed their military duties as heavy cavalry. They were descendants of the leading clans and were elected for local administrative and military offices. The rest of the Székely joined the army as common horsemen or infantry.[48] A detailed military regulation regarding the Székely was issued by King Wladislas II, in 1493. When the royal army campaigned in the east, the Székely had to join with all their available manpower. Only half were required to cross the Carpathians to the south, if the King led the army himself. Another interesting aspect is that they were entitled to wages only if the expedition was for longer than 15 days.[49]

In the second half of the sixteenth century, as Transylvania was becoming a distinct state, the Székely gradually lost their traditional freedom, and their military role and organisation were redefined. As one of the three estates of the country, the Székely had to contribute to the payment of the Turkish tribute. In 1540 they had to provide only 1,000 cavalry, the same as the nobility from the counties.[50] Very unsatisfied with the increasing demands of John Sigismund Szapolyai, the Székely rebelled in 1562. They were eventually

---

46 Ardelean, *Organizarea militară*, pp.105–106.
47 Károly Vekov, *Structuri juridico-militare și sociale la secui în evul mediu* (Cluj-Napoca: Editura Studium, 2003), pp.40–50.
48 Nathalie Kálnoky, 'L'organization militaire de la nation sicule à la fin du Moyen Âge', in Hervé Coutau-Bégarie, Ferenc Tóth (eds), *La pensée militaire hongroise à travers les siècles* (Paris: Economica, 2011), p.32.
49 Vekov, *Structuri juridico-militare*, pp.80–81.
50 *MCRT*, vol. I, p.40.

defeated and, as a consequence, the Diet of Sighişoara, held in June 1562, officially suspended their privileges as a community. Most inhabitants of the Székely Seats became serfs, some maintained a semi-privileged status in exchange for military service, while the members of the social elite had the same juridical status as the nobility.[51]

Nevertheless, the Székely continued to provide important detachments for the army of Transylvanian rulers. On the eve of the 1566 expedition in Upper Hungary, 56 Székely leaders (*primores, lófő*) joined the army of John Sigismund Szapolyai.[52] Each was accompanied by small retinues of armed servants as was the custom. The other soldiers from the Székely administrative units were also mobilised on this occasion. In Odorhei (*Udvarhely*) Seat, 378 men were registered on a muster list, 80 were absent and 39 were in the service of other nobles. The vast majority came on horseback, and only 27 were marked as infantry.[53] According to a military regulation issued the same year, all Székely horsemen were expected to have a lance (*kopja*), breastplate, helmet and shield. Those who could not afford cavalry equipment were armed with firearms (*arquebus*), sabres and wore red clothes.[54] Red became the distinctive colour of Székely soldiers throughout this period. In 1592, when Sigismund Báthory sent a small army (2,000 soldiers) into Moldavia at the request of the Ottoman Sultan, 800 infantry were recruited from the Székely Seats.[55]

It was estimated that during the Long Turkish War (1591–1606), the Székelys were able to muster about 7,000 soldiers.[56] In 1595, on the eve of his campaign in Wallachia, Sigismund Báthory restored the ancient freedoms of the Székely Estate in order to increase the size of his army. Eager to prove their military worth, 22,000 men came to the camp of Prince Sigismund near the town of Braşov. Among them 8,200 were armed with arquebuses while the rest carried spears and scythes.[57] In the following year the Székely privileges were once again annulled, and a new rebellion was brutally quelled.

The Székely suffered radical social transformation during the decades of transition from voivodeship to principality in Transylvania. From a military point of view their importance was diminished because their traditional role as defenders of the frontier was no longer relevant. Their society and their military obligations were reorganised following the pattern of the counties. The Székely elite (*primipili, lófő*) performed military service as cavalry while the

---

51 *MCRT*, vol. II, pp.202–208.

52 Károly Szabó (ed.), *Székely Oklevéltár*, vol. II (Cluj: A Magyar történelmi társulat kolozsvári bizottsága, 1876), pp.194–195.

53 Szabó (ed.), *Székely Oklevéltár*, vol.II, pp.195–206.

54 János B. Szabó, 'A székelyek katonai szerpe Erdélyben a mohácsi csatától a Habsburg uralom megszilárdulásáig (1526–1709)', in József Nagy (ed.), *A Határvédelem évszázadai Székelyföldön: Csíkszék és a Gyimesek vidéke. Szerkesztette és a jegyzékeket összeállította* (Szépvíz, 2018), p.145.

55 János B. Szabo, 'Splendid Isolation? The Military Cooperation of the Principality of Transylvania with the Ottoman Empire (1571–1688) in the Mirror of the Hungarian Historiography's Dilemmas', in Gábor Kármán, Lovro Kunčević, (ed.), *The European Tributary States of the Ottoman Empire in the Sixteenth and Seventeenth Centuries* (Leiden and Boston: Brill, 2013), p.319.

56 Makkai, *István Bocskai*, p.277.

57 Ioachim Crăciun, 'Scrisoarea lui Petru Pellérdi privitoare la ajutorul dat de Sigismund Báthory lui Mihaiu Viteazul în campania din 1595', *Anuarul Institutului de Istorie Națională*, VI (1931–1935), p.498.

other members of their community with military obligations were organised in detachments of light cavalry or infantry.

Saxons

Western European colonists, mostly of German origin, were settled on the southern and eastern borders of Transylvania during the second half of the twelfth century. After centuries of coexistence under the same privileged status they acquired a common cultural identity and were referred to as Saxons. Like the Székely, they were entrusted with the defence of the border. According to available sources it can be assumed that at least some leaders of the Saxon communities (*Gräf/Gräv*) were able to perform military service as heavy cavalry.[58] Besides defensive military obligations, the Saxons of Sibiu County had to provide a certain number of soldiers for the royal army. These obligations were established in a privilege issued by King Andrew II, in 1224. If the royal army fought inside the borders of the kingdom the Saxons sent 500 soldiers. For external campaigns their contribution was reduced to 100 soldiers, if the army was commanded by the king himself. When another commander was appointed by the king, only 50 Saxon soldiers were expected to join the royal army.[59] When their section of the border was threatened, the Saxons were able to muster a larger fighting force. In 1433 an army of 2,000 soldiers defended the southern border of Transylvania. They were billeted in the vicinity of Sibiu, but other Saxon towns (Bistriţa, Braşov) also contributed to their maintenance.[60]

The military obligations of the Transylvanian Saxons increased during the sixteenth century. Their contribution to the defence of the country was usually established during Diet sessions. According to these sources, Saxons provided detachments of infantry, usually armed with firearms (*pedites pixidari*).

Table 1. Saxon troops in the Transylvanian army 1540–1567[61]

Year	1540	1543 (Feb)	1543 (Nov)	1548	1549	1555	1556
Number of soldiers	1,000	500	1,000	2,000	2,000	1,000	2,000
Year	**1557**	**1559**	**1562**	**1565**	**1566**	**1567**	
Number of soldiers	2,000	1,000	500	1,000	2,500	3,000	

---

58 Liviu Cîmpeanu, *Universitatea Saxonă din Transilvania şi districtele româneşti aflate sub jurisdicţia ei în evul mediu şi epoca modern* (Târgu Mureş: Editura Nico, 2014), pp.33–39.

59 Cîmpeanu, *Universitatea Saxonă*, p.109.

60 Liviu Cîmpeanu, 'Obligaţii militare şi ordine de mobilizare a oraşelor săseşti din Transilvania la sfârşitul evului mediu', *Historia Urbana*, XXVII (2019), p.126.

61 Florin Nicolae Ardelean, 'Pecunia nervus belli. The Saxon University in Transylvania and its Contribution to the Military Campaign of 1566–1567', in Zoltan Iusztin (ed.), *Politics and Society in the Central and South-Eastern Europe (13th–16th centuries)* (Cluj-Napoca: Editura Mega, 2019), p.220.

Saxon troops were inspected before going on campaign and occasionally also during times of peace. In 1562 the Diet decided that the Saxon infantry should gather for regular inspections near the town of Bistriţa.[62] In 1575 the Saxon and the Székely soldiers mustered near Făgăraş or Mediaş.[63] Those who were conscripted for campaigns received regular wages. The necessary money was gathered through a special tax paid by all inhabitants of the Saxon University in Transylvania. In 1567, for example, the expedition in Upper Hungary lasted two and a half months (from early March until the middle of May). The Saxons sent 3,000 soldiers and the total amount of their wages was 24,725 florins.[64]

Saxon towns in Transylvania were important centres of weapon production. Crafting guilds, specialised in the production of swords, shields, bows, crossbows and armour were organised during the fourteenth and the fifteenth centuries. All these guilds were still active in the sixteenth century. In addition, locksmiths also produced small gunpowder weapons.[65] A significant number of gunpowder weapons were stored in the towers of Sibiu (1492/1493: 270; 1560: 681; 1567: 910; 1575: 425). The defence and provisioning of each tower was entrusted to one of the crafting guilds.[66] When the Habsburgs took control of Transylvania in 1551, they organised an arsenal in Sibiu. At the beginning of 1552 Conrad Haas was named commander of the arsenal (*Zeugwart*).[67] Large quantities of weapons, ammunition and building materials were stored within the walls of the arsenal. A significant proportion of these weapons were brought from Upper Hungary. Many of the arquebuses were produced in Nuremberg.[68] According to an inventory compiled by Conrad Haas in 1555 the arsenal of Sibiu had 45 cannons, two mortars, 186 double arquebuses, 1,327 arquebuses and 5,191 spears.[69] All these sources indicate that during the second half of the sixteenth century, Saxon towns had the largest supply of artillery and firearms in Transylvania.

When the Transylvanian army was on campaign, Saxon towns provided most of the siege and field artillery. In 1559, Chancellor Michael Csáky, issued an edict according to which the Saxon Church had to provide means of transportation (horses, carts and cart drivers) for the artillery of the Transylvanian army.[70] For the expedition initiated in spring 1567, Saxon priests had to prepare 240 horses, 10 carts and a sufficient number of cart drivers (*aurigas*) to oversee the transport. The artillery was expected to reach

---

62 *MCRT*, vol. II, p.294.

63 *MCRT*, vol. II p.570.

64 Serviciul Judeţean al Arhivelor Naţionale Sibiu (SJAN Sibiu), Socoteli consulare, nr. 87, f. 2–5.

65 Ioan Marian Ţiplic, *Bresle şi arme în Transilvania (secolele XVI–XVI)* (Bucureşti: Editura Militară, 2009), pp.59–128.

66 László Kozák-Kígyóssy Szabolcs, 'Céhes városvédelem Nagyszebenben a XV–XVI. Században', *Hadtörténelmi Közlemények* 131:4 (2018), p.841.

67 Liviu Cîmpeanu, 'The Royal Habsburg Arsenal in Sibiu (Hermannstadt, Nagyszeben) under the rule of Queen Isabella', in Ágnes Máté, Teréz Oborni, *Isabella Jagiellon Queen of Hungary (1539–1559)* (Budapest: Akadémia Kiadó, 2020), p.258.

68 Cîmpeanu, 'The Royal Habsburg Arsenal', p.262.

69 Ardelean, 'On the Foreign Mercenaries', p.124.

70 *Chronicon Fuchsio-Lupino-Oltardinum sive annales Hungarici et Transsilvanici*, vol. I, ed. Josephus Trausch (Coronae, 1847), p.61.

the camp of the army, near Cluj, in 15 days.[71] During the Long Turkish War, the military obligations of the Saxon Estate were increased. In the summer of 1595 the Saxons had to recruit a larger military force, one soldier for every 20 inhabitants, in addition to their usual detachments of infantry. Both the regular militia, the so-called 'black guards' (*pedites Saxonumqui pro veteri more nigro habitu vestiebantur*)[72] and the newly conscripted militia took part in the summer campaign of 1595 that ended with the conquest of Lipova and other Turkish fortifications in the Banat area.[73] Soon after this campaign was concluded, the Transylvanian army was gathered once more, in the vicinity of Brașov, for an expedition into Wallachia. The Saxons troops were mustered again – Sibiu: 1,000 infantry in black clothes; Brașov: 1,000 infantry in blue clothes – while the smaller towns (Mediaș, Bistrița) sent a combined detachment of 500 soldiers dressed in red and green.[74]

The Saxon towns and seats provided a large proportion of the infantry in the Transylvanian army during the second half of the sixteenth century and the beginning of the seventeenth century. Black became the distinctive colour for the clothing of Saxon soldiers although on some occasions different towns used different coloured clothes for their troops. The regular Saxon militia oscillated between 500 and 3,000 soldiers but, on exceptional occasions, a system of proportional conscription significantly increased their numbers. Saxon towns in Transylvania were usually defended by strong stone walls, even villages had fortified churches able to protect smaller communities. Weapon production and artillery was another important contribution of the Saxon community in the Transylvanian military organisation.

The Guard of the Prince

The Guard of the Prince, also referred to as the Army of the Court (*aulae militia/ aulae exercitus*) in contemporary sources, was a contingent of experienced soldiers in the service of Transylvanian rulers. They were the closest thing to a 'professional army' because they received regular wages in times of war and in times of peace. Most soldiers were recruited from the local population (nobles and commoners), but foreigners were sometimes present.

While he governed the eastern parts of the former Hungarian Kingdom, Bishop Martinuzzi had a large military retinue in his service. When he pledged loyalty to the Habsburgs, the emperor agreed to pay for 1,000 cavalry and 500 infantry as his guard.[75] In fact his personal army was much larger and included soldiers of various origins: Hungarian nobles, Transylvanian nobles, Croatian nobles (from Perušić, Bojničić, Šubić, Šušalić, Benković,

---

71 *MCRT*, vol. II, pp.329–330.
72 Wolffgangi de Bethlen, *Historia de rebus Transsylvanicis*, vol. III (Cibinii: Typis et sumptibus Martinii Hochmeister, 1785), p.585.
73 Liviu Cîmpeanu, 'Domnul fie lăudat [...] turcii au predat cetatea": Cucerirea Lipovei Otomane de către Transivlăneni în august 1595', *Historia Urbana*, XXVI (2018), pp.97–111.
74 Crăciun, 'Scrisoarea lui Petru Pellérdi', p.498.
75 ÖStA, HHSta, Hungarica AA, Fas. 61, Konv. A, f. 5.

Petričević etc.), Székely, Wallachian boyars (Drăghici Spătar and Stanciul Postelnic) and soldiers from the garrisons of Košice and Cenad, etc. A total of 4,118 soldiers were under his direct command at the height of his power.[76]

In 1556, Isabella Jagiellon and her son John Sigismund returned to Transylvania accompanied by a large retinue of Polish nobles and soldiers. Their numbers were soon increased by local nobles who chose to show their loyalty by serving as soldiers at court. While the new leadership fought to gain effective control over Transylvania, the Guard of the Court (*aulicos equites et pedites*) represented the most important part of the Transylvanian army.[77] As the war against the Habsburgs progressed the ranks of the court army were constantly increased. In 1562 the cavalry numbered 1,000 men.[78]

Various sources mention Polish and Italian mercenaries at the court of Transylvanian rulers. Soldiers from Poland were most likely recruited during the exile of Queen Isabella at the court of her brother Sigismund II Augustus. In 1556 when she regained the Transylvanian throne, Isabella was accompanied by a large retinue of Polish soldiers. A group of Italian mercenaries from Venice (100 mounted and 200 infantry), led by Giovanandrea Gromo, reached Alba Iulia in 1564 and joined the guard of John Sigismund Szapolyai.[79]

The guard was led by a supreme captain (*supremus capitaneus aulae*). During the reign of Stephen Báthory this office was initially held by Bánffy György, a member of the council and a descendent of an important Transylvanian noble family.[80] In addition, the two branches of the court army, the infantry (*peditatus aulae*) and the cavalry (*equitatus aulae*), had their own captains and officers. Nobles and Székely leaders (*primipili*) were usually chosen for such offices. In 1586, Geszthy Ferencz, future captain general of the Transylvanian army, served in the court army with a retinue of 100 horsemen.[81] Those who held important positions in the hierarchy of the Guard were trusted supporters of the ruling prince and were often rewarded with estates. They also had access to higher offices in the political, administrative and military framework of the principality.[82]

The French traveller Pierre Lescalopier visited Transylvania and the court of Alba Iulia in the summer of 1574. According to his report, the Transylvanian court was defended at the time by two companies of Polish lancers, four companies of local cavalry and 500 infantry armed with arquebuses. These soldiers were inspected on a monthly basis.[83] The estimate

---

76 Teréz Oborni, 'Fráter György szervitorainak és familiárisainak jegyzéke a Castaldo–Kódexben, 1552', *Fons*, 25: 4 (2018), pp.435–451.

77 *MCRT*, vol. II, p.86.

78 Attila Sunkó, 'Az erdélyi fejedelmek udvari hadai a 16. Században', *Levéltári Közlemények*, 69:1–2 (1998), p.106.

79 Szabó, 'The Army of the Szapolyai', pp.235–236.

80 Attila Sunkó, 'Az erdélyi fejedelmi testőrség archontológiája a XVI. Században', *Fons*, 2 (1994), p.198.

81 Magyar Tudományos Akadémia Könyvtára, Kézirattár, Budapest, Ms. 439/11, Veress Andrei, *Erdély és magyarországi kisebb történeti müvek, Geszthy Ferenc várkapitány c. értekezéshez kiegészitések*, f. 316.

82 Ardelean, 'Military Leadership', pp.348–349.

83 *Călători străini*, vol. II, p.443.

of Lescalopier is fairly accurate (about 1,100 soldiers) but in fact the size of the court army was larger. Usually, several detachments of the court army were dispatched in various parts of the country. Smaller detachments also joined campaigning armies even if the prince was not present. In December 1575 for example, 200 horsemen and 100 infantry from the court were sent to join the main army.[84] The guard of the Transylvanian prince grew in size and importance towards the end of the sixteenth century. In 1586 the court cavalry consisted of 670 mounted soldiers but after Transylvania's involvement in the Long Turkish War (1591–1606) its size was increased to 2,067.[85] The court army proved to be a very efficient political instrument. In 1594 Sigismund Báthory was able to capture and execute the leaders of the opposition (a strong faction of the nobility which opposed the idea of a war against the Turks) with the help of 400 guards (*praetorianis*).[86]

The court army took part in most battles during the Long Turkish War. In 1595, Gaspar Sibrik, captain of the court cavalry (*equitum aulae nostre capitaneis*), led 2,000 mounted soldiers during the campaign in Wallachia.[87] He commanded a detachment of the same size in the battle of Şelimbăr (28 October 1599).[88] In the same battle, Matthew Perušić, a Transylvanian noble of Croatian origin, led 600 'blue guardsmen' (*kék darabontok*) from the court infantry.[89]

Paying regular wages for a large number of troops was a heavy burden for a small state such as the Transylvanian Principality. In 1608 the Diet suggested that 500 cavalry and 500 infantry should be sufficient for the protection of the princely court in Alba Iulia.[90] The recently elected prince, Gabriel Báthory, gave his consent but in the following years he constantly increased the number of soldiers under his direct control. During his reign, many *hajdú* soldiers from the western parts of the principality and from Upper Hungary were taken into service at court. The guard became once again a political instrument, used to enforce the authoritarian rule of the last Báthory prince. The 'blue guardsmen', an elite infantry detachment of the court army, gained a particularly fearsome reputation during the occupation of Sibiu and the conflicts with the rebellious faction of Saxons.[91]

The Guard of the Prince represented a core of 'professional' soldiers in the Transylvanian army. Although foreign mercenaries (especially Polish) are sometimes mentioned in sources, most of the court army was recruited from local soldiers. The size of the guard varied between 500 and 4,000 men. Both cavalry and infantry received regular wages and were inspected periodically. Their main role was the protection of the ruler, but they were

---

84   Prodan, *Iobăgia*, vol. I, p.403.
85   Sunkó, 'Az erdélyi fejedelmek', pp.107–108.
86   Veress (ed.), *Documente*, vol. IV, pp.123–135.
87   Crăciun, 'Scrisoarea lui Petru Pellérdi', p.498.
88   Crăciun, *Cronicarul Szamosközy*, p.126.
89   Sándor Szilágyi, (ed.), 'Szamosközy István történeti maradványai 1566–1603', vol. II 1598–1599, Monumenta Hungariae Historica 2, Scriptores 28 (Budapest: Magyar Tudományos Akadémia, 1876), p.323.
90   *MCRT*, vol. VI, p.94.
91   *Memorialul lui Nagy Szabó Ferencz*, pp.149–150.

also mobilised, entirely or partially, for expeditions inside or beyond the borders of Transylvania.

Hajdús

The *hajdús* were a distinct social group, with a strong military character, who inhabited the borderlands of Hungary and Transylvania. They are first mentioned in historical sources at the end of the fifteenth century and their main occupation was cattle husbandry and trade.[92] As the Ottoman threat advanced, the *hajdús* became very skilled in irregular warfare, typical for border regions (raids, ambushes etc.). In 1514 many of them joined the rebellion of Dózsa György and fought against royal authority. After the rebellion was defeated, the King and the Diet attempted to disband the *hajdús* (*besliae*), but they were unsuccessful.[93] Their numbers increased steadily after the battle of Mohács (1526). After the division of the Hungarian kingdom some of them remained in Habsburg-controlled regions (Upper Hungary) while others lived in the territories administered by Transylvanian rulers (the Banat region and Bihor County). The so-called 'royal *hajdús*' were employed in local garrisons and received wages. The 'free *hajdús*' were sometimes taken into service for military campaigns but mostly adhered to their traditional lifestyle of raiding and cattle trading.[94] In his book about the exploits of General Castaldo in Transylvania, Ascanio Centorio describes the *hajdús* as excellent infantry who imitate the Turks in respect of their weapons, equipment and fighting style.[95]

Several sources mention the *hajdús* as part of the Transylvanian army during the Long Turkish War (1591–1606). In the first phase of the conflict they were very active in the Banat area where they organised frequent raids into the territories of the Ottoman province of Timișoara. A group of 4,000 'free *hajdús*' settled in the vicinity of Lipova fortress after it was conquered by the troops of Sigismund Báthory in 1595.[96] They were also present in the vicinity of Caransebeș and posed a constant threat to neighbouring Turkish territories. Their raids reached the Danube area and beyond.[97]

The highlight of *hajdú* history was the rebellion of Stephen Bocskai, Transylvanian Prince and Hungarian King (1604–1606). They were the most numerous and trustworthy troops in the army of Bocskai and fought with fierce determination against the Catholic Habsburgs who had taken measures against freedom of religion(most *hajdús* were followers of the Reformation). As a reward for their faithful service the *hajdús* gained privileged status, and they were free men exempted from paying taxes in exchange for military service. A document issued on 12 December 1605 referred to 9,254 soldiers

---

92 Engel, *Regatul*, pp.341–342.
93 Prodan, *Iobăgia*, vol. I, p.165.
94 Makkai, 'István Bocskai', p.277.
95 Centorio, *Comentarii*, p.104.
96 Veress (ed.), *Documente*, vol. V, p.23.
97 Veress (ed.), *Documente*, vol. V, p.64.

Stephen Bocskai and his *hajdú* soldiers in 1605.

who were given eight villages in Bihor County. In the following year other groups, 300 and then another 700, were given a similar privileged status.[98]

Their recently won freedom was threatened by the nobility after the death of Bocskai in 1606. The *hajdús* rebelled and threatened the stability of both Royal Hungary and Transylvania.[99] Their saviour was the new Transylvanian prince, Gabriel Báthory, with whom they signed an agreement at Debrecen, in February 1608. He guaranteed their privileged status and in exchange the *hajdús* became his loyal soldiers.[100] The leader of the *hajdús*, Nagy András, became one of the most trusted of Báthory's councillors and helped him with the occupation of Sibiu and the campaign in Wallachia in December 1610. In 1612 he besieged Braşov with 6,000 *hajdús* but was unable to capture the town. One year later when he returned to Transylvania from Upper Hungary, he was captured and executed by Báthory who suspected him of treason.[101]

The *hajdús* became one of the most important groups in the composition of the Transylvanian army at the beginning of the seventeenth century. They played a vital role in the rebellion of Stephen Bocskai and during the authoritarian rule of Gabriel Báthory. Most *hajdús* usually fought as infantry but they also formed cavalry detachments. They were a versatile military group, most efficient in irregular warfare.

98 Makkai, 'István Bocskai', p.293.
99 András Komáromy, 'Az 1607-iki hajdúlázadás történetéhez', *Hadtörténelmi Közlemények*, IV (1891), pp.226–233.
100 *MCRT*, vol. V, pp.570–574.
101 Kraus, *Cronica*, p.22.

Boyars, Guardsmen, Arquebusiers and Other Social Groups with Military Obligations

The complex structure of early modern Transylvanian society included several intermediary groups which can be defined as semi-privileged, not part of the 'true nobility' (*una eademque nobilitas*) but not peasants either. These groups benefited from tax exemptions and other benefices in exchange for military service. Most of them lived on the fiscal estate (the lands of the ruling prince) and were concentrated in the vicinity of important fortifications.

The boyars from Făgăraș district, representatives of the Romanian social elite on the southern border of Transylvania, were at first recognised as true nobles but, during the era of the principality, they were gradually transformed into a semi-privileged group with military obligations. Their status was recognised only within the limits of their district (*Țara Făgărașului*).[102] The boyars went to war on horseback and their main offensive weapon was the lance. In the second half of the sixteenth century, Făgăraș district contributed with 200 soldiers when the Transylvanian army went on campaign. When their section of the border was threatened, all those capable of bearing arms were expected to mobilise.[103] In his will, issued in 1585 at Niepołomice, King Stephen Báthory gave Făgăraș to his kinsman Balthazar Báthory. A new military regulation was drafted on this occasion. According to this document all boyars had the obligation to join the army of the prince during campaigns and an additional detachment of 200 cavalry and 100 infantry was mobilised from this region.[104]

Sometimes Transylvanian rulers rewarded faithful soldiers with the status of guardsmen (*darabont*). They received land plots, usually in the vicinity of important fortifications. Guardsmen were exempted from paying most taxes and from performing work obligations in exchange for military duties. In 1583, Stephen Báthory rewarded one of his Transylvanian soldiers, Szásznyiresi Orosz Mihály, with the status of free guardsmen on the estate of Gherla fortress.[105] Although the document doesn't mention it specifically, he was probably one of those who accompanied Báthory to Poland and fought in the siege of Gdansk (1577) and the Livonian campaigns against the Russian ruler Ivan IV, the Terrible (1577–1582). This is probably the origin of the second surname of the Transylvanian soldier's, Orosz, which translates as 'the Russian'.

Arquebusiers (*pedites pixidari, sclopetari, gyalogpuskások*) were also a social and military group present on the fiscal estates of Transylvania. Their social status was similar to that of the guardsmen, and they performed a similar role. A specific feature of this group was the use of gunpowder

---

102 Ionuţ Costea, *Solam virtutem et nomen bonum. Nobilitate, Etnie, Regionalism în Transilvania Princiară* (Cluj-Napoca: Editura Argonaut, 2005), pp.181–183.

103 David Prodan, 'Boieri şi vecini în Ţara Făgăraşului în sec. XVI–XVII', in *Din istoria Transilvaniei. Studii şi evocări* (Bucureşti: Editura Enciclopedică, 1991), pp.37–38.

104 Endre Veress (ed.), *Báthory István erdélyi fejedelem és lengyel király levelezése*, vol. II (1576–1586) (Koloszvár: Erdélyi Tudományos Intézet, 1944), p.299.

105 Veress (ed.), *Báthory István*, vol. II, p.234.

weapons. In 1581, Voivode Cristofer Báthory awarded a collective privilege to the men settled on the Gilău estate, in central Transylvania. Their main obligation was to join the army whenever the ruler requested it. In exchange they were exempted from any tax and work obligations, including contribution towards the Turkish tribute.[106]

In 1590, 93 men lived in the villages of the Gherla estate. They were exempted from all taxes and work obligations and in exchange they had to join the army of the Transylvanian ruler, armed with a good arquebus and a sabre. Sons inherited their father's status. They were subjected only to the authority of the prince or his appointed military commanders. In case of immediate danger they were required to join the garrison of Gherla fortress.[107] In the abovementioned situations these arquebus-armed men are regarded primary as elements of the filed army. However, sources also mention these men in border areas. On the estate of Oradea fortress, on the western border of Transylvania, they are mentioned by sources alongside infantry and cavalry freemen. In many cases the men were appointed directly by the ruling prince. In 1597, Sigismund Báthory issued a document in favour of brothers Filip and Toma Botta, who were recognised as part of this group and were given a house on the vast estate of Oradea.[108]

Another social group with military obligations were the freemen (*libertini*, *szabados*). They also lived mostly on fiscal estates and were exempted from certain taxes and obligations. However, not all freemen performed military service. Some of them were craftsmen or performed other activities such as fishing, hunting, mining etc. Even serfs who were recently settled on deserted plots and were temporarily exempted from taxes appear sometimes in documents as freemen.[109] The conscription records of Chioar estate register freemen separately from guardsmen and the arquebusiers. In 1566, 46 freemen lived in 18 different villages of this large estate. It is unclear if all

Christopher Báthory, voivode of Transylvania 1576–1581, *Trachten-Kabinett von Siebenbürgens*, 1729. (The National Museum of Transylvanian History, Cluj-Napoca, Romania)

---

106 Prodan, *Iobăgia*, vol. I, p.411.
107 Prodan, *Iobăgia*, vol. II, p.193.
108 Magyar Nemzeti Levéltár Országos Levéltára (MNL OL), F 15, Kolozsmonostori Konvent Országos Levéltára – Protocolla, libri regi et stilionaria, 14, f. 16–17.
109 Prodan, *Iobăgia*, vol. I, pp.203–209.

of them had military obligations or if some were involved in other types of activities.[110] Later, in 1603, their number had increased to 87.[111]

During the Middle Ages, the Romanian social elite of Transylvania was partially integrated in the noble class of the Hungarian kingdom (*una eademque nobilitas*). Some of those who didn't make the transition were able to maintain a semi-privileged status. Estate conscriptions and other type of administrative documents mention various smaller groups or individuals which performed military service, under the names of *voievozi, cnezi, crainici* and *juzi* (village reeves). A conscription record of the Hunedoara estate, on the south-western border of Transylvania, mentions 177 *cnezi* and *crainici* who performed military service on horseback. Some of them are associated to hussars and had a similar status to that of military freemen.[112] *Voievozii* had enough resources to equip themselves as cavalrymen. In addition to their military obligations they were also tasked with gathering taxes and other contributions.[113]

The Banat of Lugoj and Caransebeş was a region where the *cnezi* were able to maintain their privileged status. At the beginning of the seventeenth century, Prince Gabriel Báthory confirmed the collective privilege of the nobles and *cnezi* from the town of Lugoj and eight other districts in its vicinity. The privilege was granted by the Hungarian King Ladislaus V, in 1457, and was later confirmed by Queen Isabella Jagiellon in 1551. The document explicitly mentions their military merits in defending the border area from Turkish raids and invasion.[114] Village reeves (*juzi*) were involved in various aspects of military organisation, such as overseeing the mobilisation of the local peasant militia, communicating military information to higher authorities and gathering supplies for the army.[115]

This large variety of semi-privileged groups played an important role in the defensive system of Transylvania. Their historical evolution is strictly connected to the fiscal estate (lands of the ruling prince) and the network of fortifications that ensured the defence of the country. They share many similarities in terms of social status. Distinctions are determined by ethnic origin and fighting style. Some of these soldiers (for example the arquebus-armed troops) were also mobilised for external campaigns and bolstered the ranks of the princely banner.

110 Meteş, Ştefan, *Vieaţa agrară, economică a românilor din Ardeal şi Ungaria. Documente contemporane 1508–1820*, vol. I (Bucureşti: Tipografia "România Nouă" Th. Voinea, 1921), pp.194–198.

111 Meteş, *Viaţa agrară*, p.216.

112 Prodan, *Iobăgia*, vol. I, pp.198–200.

113 Prodan, *Iobăgia*, vol. I, p.500.

114 Veress (ed.), *Documente*, vol. VIII, p.61.

115 Livia Magina, *Instituţia judelui sătesc în Principatul Transilvaniei* (Cluj-Napoca: Editura Mega, 2014), pp.245–248.

3

Fortifications, Artillery and Garrisons

The Western Frontier of Transylvania

The Transylvanian Principality inherited a vast network of fortifications built during previous centuries. In the Middle Ages, Hungarian kings were concerned with organising a strong frontier on the eastern and southern borders of the province, through 'military colonisations' and by building fortresses.[1] When Transylvania became a distinct state, during the second half of the sixteenth century, the western frontier was the region with the most intense military activity. The border with Habsburg Hungary and the Ottoman Empire changed frequently, mostly to the detriment of the Principality.

Various fortifications can be distinguished based on architectural, institutional or functional criteria. Border fortresses (usually situated on the fiscal estates), fortified towns, castles and fortified churches were some of the most common types of fortifications throughout Transylvania in the sixteenth and seventeenth centuries.

The most recent innovations in the field of military architecture, the bastion fortifications (*trace italienne*), reached Transylvania quickly. During the second half of the sixteenth century, a considerable number of Italian architects and engineers (*fundatores*) travelled to Transylvania and shared their expertise in the art of fortress building. Among them were Alessandro Clippa, Alessandro da Urbino, Sigismondo da Pratovecchio, Felice da Pisa, Ottavio Baldigara, Francesco da Pozzo and Simone Genga.[2]

Timișoara

The western border of Transylvania changed frequently during the second half of the sixteenth century and the beginning of the seventeenth century.

---

1   Adrian A. Rusu, Castelarea carpatică: Fortificațiile și cetățile din Transilvania și teritoriile învecinate (sec. XIII–XIV) (Cluj Napoca: Editura Mega, 2005), pp.295–312.

2   Klára Kovács, 'Fortresses-Building in sixteenth Century Transylvania. The Recruitment of Labour Force', *Transylvanian Review*, Vol. XXI, Supplement No. 2 (2012), pp.163–170.

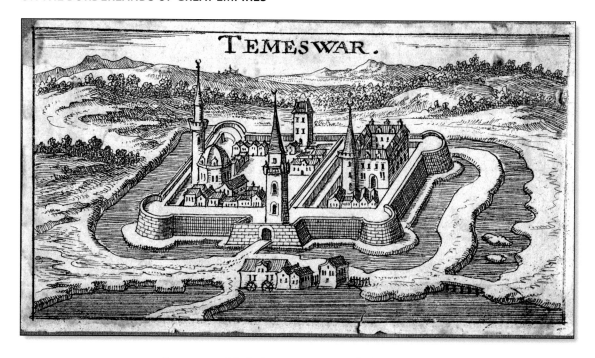

Timișoara in the seventeenth century, Christoff Riegel, *Das Ehemals gedrückte, vom Türken berückte, nun Trefflich erquickte Königreich Hungarn*, Frankfurt, Leipzig, 1688. (National Museum of Banat, Timișoara, România)

Fortresses with their estates or even whole counties were conquered or changed sides willingly between the Ottomans, the Habsburgs and Transylvania. The first radical territorial change took place on the southern sector of the western frontier, in 1552, when Timișoara and other fortifications from the Banat region were conquered by the Ottomans. By that time, Timișoara was already a modern fortification with bastions, made of wood and earth. Its defensive potential was increased by the surrounding marshland which made any potential siege attempt very difficult.[3] This important territorial loss occurred while Transylvania was under temporary Habsburg control (1551–1556) and was a direct consequence of this political change. The first attempt to take Timișoara was made in November 1551. On this occasion, the fortress was defended by a large force of 3,570 soldiers, both locals and Habsburg foreign mercenaries (German and Spanish). Eventually the Turks were forced to retreat because of the rainy weather.[4] A new Ottoman army led by Kara Ahmed Pasha, besieged Timișoara in the summer of 1552. István Losonci, commander of the defending forces, had only 2,300 soldiers at his disposal, among which were 450 Spanish mercenaries.[5] The summer was hot and dry, and the Ottomans were able to effectively encircle the fortress. A section of the curtain wall collapsed under sustained artillery fire. Losonci decided to surrender under the condition that he and his soldiers would be allowed to leave the fortress unharmed. The Turks agreed to these terms but while the garrison left Timișoara, an incident occurred and Losonci,

---

3   Gheorghe Anghel, *Cetăți medievale din Transilvania* (București: Editura Meridiane, 1972), p.92; Mihail Guboglu, Mustafa Ali Mehmet (eds), *Cronici turcești privind Țările Române*, vol. I (București: Editura Academiei R.S.R., 1966), p.284.

4   Károly Czimer, 'Temesvár megvétele 1551–1552' I, *Hadtörténelmi Közlemények*, VI (1893), p.34.

5   Czimer, 'Temesvár megvétele' III, p.319.

together with some of his men, were killed by Turkish soldiers. These events were described in a contemporary epic song by Sebestyén Tióndi Lantos, entitled *Az vég Temesvárban Losonci Istvánnak haláláról*.[6] Many other smaller fortifications from the Banat area were lost during this period. The occupied territories were organised into a distinct Ottoman province (*vilayet*).[7]

Lugoj and Caransebeș

Lugoj and Caransebeș were the most important fortifications in the mountainous area of the Banat. According to Ottoman sources they were both conquered in 1552 and given back to the rightful rulers of Transylvania in the following years.[8] Together with other settlements in the area they formed a distinct administrative unit known as the Banat of Lugoj and Caransebeș. This section of the western frontier was supervised by a *ban*, an important official in the military hierarchy of the Transylvanian army.[9] Both Lugoj and Caransebeș were important urban settlements protected by fortifications.[10] Caransebeș was surrounded by a stone wall and a dry moat. General Castaldo planned to modernise these fortifications, but no bastions were built during the sixteenth century. The *ban* had a significant retinue of 500 horsemen under his command. Other important fortifications in this area were Mehadia and Jdioara.[11]

Lipova

Lipova was another important fortification conquered by the Turks in 1552. Situated on the southern banks of the Mureș River, Lipova consisted of a rectangular stone castle protected by an additional system of earth and wooden walls. The outer wall was constructed in a modern manner with angular bastions.[12] It was a large fortification, able to host a large garrison. According to Ottoman sources, the fortress was defended by a permanent detachment of soldiers at all times: 1,554 infantry (*müsztahfiz*) and two high ranking officers, 27 artillerymen (*topci*), three carpenters, 115 *azab* light infantry and 43 *martalos* infantry.[13] During the Long Turkish War (1591–1606) the most important strategic objective of the Transylvanian army was to retake the Banat region. Timișoara was besieged twice, in 1596 and 1597, without success. However, the troops of Prince Sigismund Báthory were able

6   Márta A. Ghezzo, *Epic Songs of Sixteenth–Century Hungary* (Budapest: Akadémiai Kiadó, 1989), pp.143–145.
7   Cristina Feneșan, *Vilayetul Timișoara (1552–1716)* (Timișoara: Editura Ariergarda, 2014), pp.19–29.
8   Cristina Feneșan-Bulgaru, 'Problema instaurării dominației otomane asupra Banatului Lugojului și Caransebeșului', *Banatica*, IV (1977), pp.223–238.
9   Dragoș Lucian Țigău, 'Between Ephemerality and Fiction. Addenda to the History of the Bans of Caransebes and Lugoj', *Banatica*, 26:2 (2016), pp.351–367.
10   Liviu Groza, 'Cetatea Caransebeș – câteva precizări cronologice', *Bantica*, 12–2 (1993), pp.89–99.
11   Giovannandrea Gromo, *Compendio di tutto il regno posseduto dal re Giovanni Transilvano et di tutte le cose notabili d'esso regno (Sec. XVI)*, ed. Aurel Decei (Alba Iulia: Tip. "Alba", 1945), p.20.
12   Anghel, *Cetăți medievale*, p.119.
13   Klára Hegyi, *A török hódoltság várai és várkatonasága*, vol. III (Budapest: História: MTA Történettudományi Intézete, 2007), pp.1447–1450.

to conquer Lipova after a siege that lasted just four days.[14] In the following years this fortress was the jumping-off point for many raids that targeted the neighbouring Ottoman territories. Under the command of Captain György Borbély, the garrison of Lipova frequently fought the Ottoman troops from the border area. It is very hard to assess the size of the garrison during this period. The fortress was probably defended by several hundred soldiers but, in case of immediate danger, their numbers were increased by other troops from the border area. Contemporary sources mention large detachments of Serbians (*Rasciani*) and *hajdús* who were very proficient in the ways of irregular warfare. Chronicler István Szamosközi also mentions a detachment of Scottish mercenaries (about 300 men) which had arrived in Transylvania from Danzig. In 1596, 143 of these Scotsmen were sent to reinforce the garrison of Lipova.[15] The fortress remained under Transylvanian control until 1616 when it was returned to the Ottomans.

Ineu

Further north, beyond the Mureș valley, the defensive line was continued by the fortifications of Șiria and Ineu. A castle was built at Ineu in the second half of the fifteenth century as a residence of the Losonci family. Later, the fortification was expanded and modernised according to the new principles of military architecture. In 1552, the Turkish conquest of Banat reached the area beyond the Mureș River, including Ineu. For more than four decades, with a small interruption in 1565 when it was occupied by Habsburg troops for a short while, Ineu remained under Ottoman control. In 1595, the armies of the Transylvanian Prince Sigismund Báthory were able to retake this fortification.[16] At the end of the 'Long Turkish War' Ineu was firmly under Transylvanian control, although the constant fighting in the area had a strong demographic and economic impact. According to a conscription notice made in 1605, the estate of the fortress consisted of ten settlements. Many dwellings were deserted, and the Transylvanian officials were able to register only 90 families who had very little in the way of possessions. According to this document, Ineu was a modern fortification, consisting of an inner citadel with three bastions and on outer wall, defended by five additional bastions. The fortress was well supplied with provisions, weapons and ammunition. Arquebuses, muskets (65 pieces) and janissary rifled muskets were recorded in the inventory of the fortress. The artillery consisted mostly of light bronze and iron guns (falconets and bombards). Close combat weapons like two handed swords, halberds, lances and various elements of plate armour (mostly of German origin) were also recorded.[17]

---

14 Cîmpeanu, 'Domnul fie lăudat', pp.97–111.

15 Szilágyi (ed.), 'Szamosközy István' vol. IV, p.56.

16 Eugen Glück, 'Contribuții cu privire la istoricul cetății de la Ineu', *Ziridava*, XIII (1981), pp.131–138.

17 Adrian Magina, 'Conscripția și inventarul bunurilor cetății Ineu în anul 1605', *Banatica*, 21 (2011), pp.90–104.

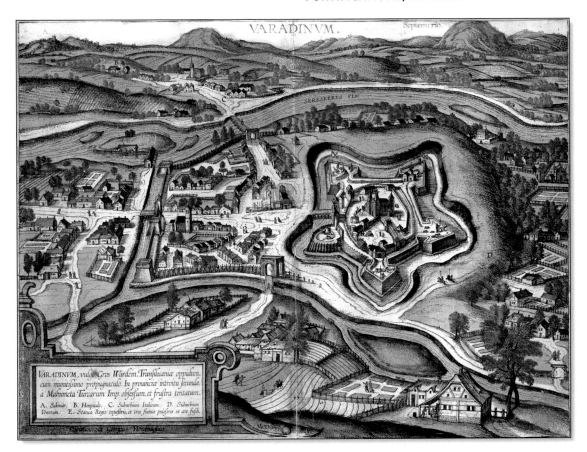

Oradea

Oradea was the centrepiece of the Transylvanian western defensive line. The medieval fortification defended a cathedral and the palace of the bishop.[18] In the last year of his reign, John Sigismund Szapolyai initiated the construction of a modern fortification. It had a pentagonal plan. The five bastions and the defensive walls had the same height of nine to 10 metres. Ottavio Baldigara was among the Italian architects who coordinated the construction of this important Transylvanian fortification. The large market town situated in the vicinity of the fortress was also encircled by a wooden rampart.[19]

The construction of this fortification was one of the most expensive and ambitious projects of the Transylvanian Principality, which took several decades to complete. Although Oradea had a huge estate consisting of 47 villages and two market towns, its income was not enough to cover the construction costs. The Diet approved yearly contributions 'for the necessities of Oradea fortress' that were paid by the whole country.[20] The captain of Oradea was one of the most important positions in the military hierarchy. This office was usually entrusted to representatives of leading noble families. Stephen Báthory and Stephen Bocskai held this military

The fortress of Oradea and its surroundings in 1598, illustrated by Georg Hoefnagel. (Țării Crișurilor Museum, Oradea, Romania)

---

18   Marta, *Cetatea Oradiei*, pp.35–45.
19   Anghel, *Cetăți medievale*, p.117.
20   Ardelean, *Organizarea militară*, p.141.

office before becoming rulers of Transylvania.[21] The authority of the captain of Oradea extended over four other smaller fortifications in Bihor County, Sákár, Bajom, Sarkad and Beliu.[22]

There is little information about the size of the regular garrison during this period. Sources provide detailed information on this matter when describing important sieges, but during such events the number of defenders was increased. Oradea was besieged by a significant Turkish force in 1598. According to the report drafted by the Habsburg commander of the fortification, Melchior Redern (Rödern), the fortress was defended by four companies of German infantry (*knechte*), 350 guardsmen (*trabanten*), a mixed contingent of German and Hungarian cavalry (300 men), one hussar company, several companies of Silesian heavy cavalry (*schleisischen pferdt*), 150 *hajdús* and some French mercenaries.[23] In the first part of the Long Turkish War (1591–1606), Transylvania and the Habsburgs fought as allies, and this is the reason why the local garrison from Oradea was enforced by significant Habsburg contingents during the 1598 siege.

Besides Oradea, other important fortifications in Bihor County were Adrian, Finiş, Cheresig, Diosig, Pocsaj, Pomezeu, Săcuieni, Şinteu, Sâniob and Şoimi. Some were part of the fiscal estate while others were owned by local noble families.[24]

Şimleu

During the fifteenth century, the Transylvanian branch of the Báthory family constructed a castle on one of their most import estates, Şimleu, in Crasna County. In time it became their main residence, and the family was known as Báthory of Şimleu (*Somlyai Báthory*). Their most renowned descendent was Stephen Báthory, ruler of Transylvania (1571–1586) and Polish-Lithuanian King (1576–1586). In the second half of the sixteenth century, a modern fortification with four bastions was built around the medieval castle.[25] In 1594, Şimleu fortress and its large domain (two market towns and 47 villages) were integrated in the fiscal estate of the country and played an important role in the defence of the western border. An inventory drafted on this occasion, shows that the fortress was well supplied with weapons and gunpowder: one heavy gun, seven bombards, 97 arquebuses, six rifled muskets, 6,600 arquebus shot, 619 bombard shot, 34 barrels of gunpowder and numerous lances, spears and arrows.[26] The permanent garrison was rather small, only 10 guardsmen were mentioned in the same document.

21 Margit Balás, *A váradi kapitányság története* (Nagyvárad: Láng József Könyvnyomdája, 1917), pp.18–19.

22 *MCRT*, vol. III, p.402.

23 Beda Dudik, 'Rödern Menyhért császári tábornagy tudósítasa Nagy-Várad 1598-iki ostromoltatásáról', *Történelmi tár*, 1 (1878), pp.106–108.

24 Gheorghe Gorun, 'Fortificaţii bihorene în lupta pentru apărarea autonomiei Transilvaniei', *Muzeul Naţional*, V(1981), p.166.

25 Rudolf Wolf, 'Cetatea Şimleului. Schiţă monografică', *Acta Musei Porolissensis*, V (1981), pp.400–403.

26 András Kovács, 'Szilágysomlyó vára a 16. Században', *Dolgozatok az Erdélyi Múzeum érem- és régiségtárából*, VIII (2013), pp.95–106.

Nevertheless, 113 free guardsmen (*szabados drabant*) and 19 free horsemen lived in the nearby settlements and, if necessary, they could have easily joined the resident garrison.[27] Maintaining a large force of semi-privileged soldiers on the estate of the fortress was cheaper than paying monthly wages for a large permanent garrison. Transylvanian rulers applied this strategy on all their fortress estates.

In the following decades the number of soldiers on the estate of Şimleu fortress was increased. In 1610, Prince Gabriel Báthory settled 128 soldiers from his 'field army' in a village of Şimleu estate. Although their main responsibility was to join the army of the prince on campaigns, they also had the obligation to defend the border.[28]

Chioar

Further north, the western defensive line was continued by the fortress of Chioar. The first phase of the fortification dates from the thirteenth century. Chioar was among the fortresses built by Hungarian royalty as a reaction to the Mongol invasion of 1241. In the fourteenth and fifteenth centuries, the fortress was in the possession of prominent noble families from the area like Laczkfi and Dragfi.[29] In the second half of the sixteenth century, Chioar fortress and its large domain (one market town and 66 villages) were included in the fiscal estate.[30]

Although Transylvanian rulers preferred to exercise direct control over the most important strategic points on the western frontier, large fortifications were sometimes given to faithful nobles. Chioar, for example, was donated to Cristofor Hagymássy in 1568.[31] He was a loyal supporter of John Sigismund Szapolyai, captain of Huszt fortress and captain general of the Transylvanian army. Hagymássy was an experienced military commander and thus, this gift did not weaken the western frontier. It was a political gesture meant to improve relations with an influential member of the nobility and to decentralise the burden of defending the frontier.

In 1578 Chioar passed once more into the hands of the ruling prince and remained in the possession of the Báthory family until 1600. In the chaos that enveloped Transylvania during the last phase of the Long Turkish War, the fortress was conquered by the Habsburg commander of Satu Mare fortress, Michael Székely.[32] Later, in 1615, the fortress was returned to the Transylvanian Prince Gabriel Bethlen, after long negotiations with the representatives of the Habsburgs.[33]

---

27 MNL OL, Urbaria et Conscriptiones, E 156 - a,Fasc. 113, No. 005, f. 1–90; Prodan, *Iobăgia*, vol. II, pp.596–599.
28 MNL OL, F 7 Armales, nr. 29.
29 Valer Hossu, *Nobilimea Chioarului* (Baia Mare: Biblioteca Judeţeană "Petre Dulfu", 2003), pp.17–19.
30 Prodan, *Iobăgia*, vol. I, p.593.
31 *MCRT*, vol. II, p.310.
32 Veress (ed.), *Documente*, vol. VI, p.188.
33 *MCRT*, vol. VII, pp.274–277.

Satu Mare

The frontier between Transylvania and Royal Hungary changed frequently during the second half of the sixteenth century. One of the most disputed fortifications in this area was Satu Mare. Even before the early modern fortification was built, Satu Mare was considered an important strategic point on the Someş River. In 1526 the market town was given to the Báthory family. They increased the defensive potential of the settlement by creating an artificial branch of the river. When their work was done, the market town and the site where the fortress was to be built in the following decades was encircled by waters.[34]

In 1564, when Satu Mare was occupied by the Habsburgs, Cesare Baldigara drafted three distinct plans for the construction of a modern fortress.[35] The work on the new fortification did not start right away because Stephen Báthory, captain general of the Transylvanian army at the time, was able retake this region for a short while. A counter-offensive led by the Habsburg general Lazarus Schwendi brought Satu Mare under Habsburg control again at the beginning of 1565. General Schwendi was among those who favoured a pentagonal plan for the new fortification, inspired by the fortress of Neuhedin (Hesdin).[36] The main building materials were wood and earth. The curtain walls and the five bastions were reinforced with large wooden logs. Each section of the curtain wall was 170 metres long while the sides of the bastions were 95 metres long. The construction lasted until 1573. Paolo Cattaneo, another Italian architect in Habsburg service, supervised the last phase of the construction.[37]

For the Habsburgs, the fortress of Satu Mare was one of the most important strategic points on the eastern edge of their frontier with the Ottomans. Transylvanian rulers considered it as part of their political heritage and made constant efforts to retake it by military or diplomatic means. A large estate, consisting of 186 villages and market towns, inhabited by 6,540 serfs and their families, provided for the needs of this important fortification.[38]

Information about the size of the garrison and artillery is provided by documents issued by Habsburg authorities while the fortification was under their control. In 1577, Satu Mare was defended by 500 German infantry (*knechte*), 100 cavalry, 25 guardsmen (local infantry) and 32 gunners. Satu Mare was among the few Habsburg fortifications in the area defended by heavy artillery. An inventory made in 1577 mentions 11 heavy guns (four *Singern* and seven *Quartirschlange*), several types of lighter guns (two *Falconi*,

---

34 Adalbert Burai, 'Despre cetatea de tip italian din Satu Mare', *Studii şi Comunicări. Satu Mare* I (1969), pp.129–130.

35 György Domokos, 'Egy Itáliai várfundáló mester Magyarországon a XVI. század második felében: Ottavio Baldigara élete és tevékenysége', *Hadtörténelmi Közlemények* (4) (1998), pp.824, 835–836.

36 Kovács P. Klára, 'Planimetria cetăţii bastionare de la Satu Mare în context European', *Ars Transsilvaniae* XIX (2009), p.28.

37 Burai, 'Despre cetatea de tip italian', p.131.

38 Marius Diaconescu (ed.), *Izvoare de antroponimie şi demografie istorică. Conscripţiile cetăţii Sătmar din 1569–1570* (Cluj-Napoca: Editura Mega, 2012), p.x.

one *Scharfetindl*, 10 *Haubitz*, two *Morse* and 14 organ guns), and 534 hand-held gunpowder weapons.[39]

The fortress remained under Habsburg authority during the last decades of the sixteenth century. When the rebellion of Stephan Bocskai began in 1604, Satu Mare was among the few Habsburg garrisons who opposed the rebel army. The fortress was besieged by a large force and surrendered on 16 January 1605.[40] In 1606, after the death of Stephan Bocskai, the fortress and the County of Satu Mare were regained by the Habsburgs following diplomatic negotiations.[41]

Hust

The fortress of Hust (today Хуст in Ukraine) was built on a high ridge, in the vicinity of the Tisa River. Situated in Maramureș County, this fortification was meant to protect the Transylvanian border with Habsburg Hungary and Poland. Bastions were built in addition to the medieval fortification during the second half of the sixteenth century.[42] The Hust estate was rather small, consisting of only 16 settlements.[43]

Transylvanian rulers and the Habsburg kings of Hungary frequently fought for the control of this important border fortification. According to the peace treaty of Speyer (1570) signed between Maximilian II of Habsburg and John Sigismund Szapolyai, Hust belonged to Transylvania.[44] In 1599, during the Long Turkish War, the fortress was occupied by a Habsburg garrison.[45] Stephen Bocskai regained Hust in 1604 and left it as a personal heritage to Bálint Drugeth of Homonna, an influential noble from Upper Hungary, in 1606. Two years later, in 1608, Prince Gabriel Báthory bought the fortress for the considerable sum of 30,000 florins.[46]

The defence of Hust was ensured by a small resident garrison and various groups of semi-privileged soldiers settled in the surrounding villages. An inventory of the fortress elaborated in 1550 mentions only light artillery (falconets and mortars), arquebuses (*pixidis barbatis*) and smaller handguns (*pixidis manuales*).[47] The captain of the fortress paid regular wages to a small retinue of 16 horsemen, 33 soldiers, three officers, four night guards, one gunner and one trumpeter. The vice-captain was usually accompanied by four mounted guards.[48] In most cases the captain of Hust fortress also held the office of count (*ispán*) of Maramureș and thus was entitled to command

---

39   Burai, 'Despre cetatea de tip italian', pp.142–143.

40   Makkai, 'István Bocskai', pp.281–290.

41   Lukinich, *Erdély területiváltozásai*, p.209.

42   Alajos Deschmann, 'Huszt vára – A Máramarosi sóbányák őre', *Műemlékvédelem*, 35:3 (1991), pp.160–162.

43   MNL OL, Urbaria et Conscriptiones, E 156 – a, – Fasc. 174, No. 026, f. 1–31.

44   Octavian Tătar, 'Tratatul de la Speyer (1570) dintre Maximilian al II-lea și Ioan Sigismund Zápolya și statutul politico-teritorial al Transilvaniei pe plan european', *Annales Universitatis Apulensis.Historica*, 7 (2003), p.196.

45   Veress (ed.), *Documente*, vol. VI, p.2.

46   Veress (ed.), *Documente*, vol. VIII, p.150.

47   MNL OL HU MNL OL, Urbaria et Conscriptiones, E 156 – a, Fasc. 075, No. 040, f. 2.

48   Prodan, *Iobăgia*, vol. I, p.502.

additional troops (200 cavalry and 400 infantry).[49] In 1594, Gaspar Kornis, who held both offices at the time, was able to mobilise up to 1,000 soldiers and intended to oppose a much larger Tatar force that was attempting to cross the mountains into Hungary.[50]

The western frontier of Transylvania was a very unstable region from a political point of view. Territorial changes occurred often as three powers (Ottomans, Habsburgs and Transylvanians) fought for its control. Fortifications were the most prized objectives in this protracted competition for territorial expansion. Both military and diplomatic means were employed to secure control over these important strategic points. Fortresses, with their large estates, also represented an important demographic and economic resource.

Border fortifications in Transylvania share many similarities. Most of them were under the direct authority of the elected ruler and were considered part of the fiscal estate. Each of the abovementioned fortresses were surrounded by an estate, consisting of villages and market towns, meant to support the needs of the local garrison and the administrative apparatus. They were usually positioned in the vicinity of an important river (Lipova on the Mureş River; Oradea on the Criş River; Satu Mare on the Someş River; Chioar on the Lăpuş River, and Huston the Tisa River). Fortresses built on high ground, like Chioar and Hust, had an irregular plan, while those built on flat land followed a regular pattern, usually pentagonal (Oradea, Satu Mare for example). Both Transylvanian and Habsburg authorities invested in the modernisation of the defensive system by building new fortresses or by adding bastions to the existing medieval fortifications. Small permanent garrisons aided by various groups of semi-privileged soldiers (guardsmen, arquebusiers etc.) were responsible for defending border fortifications. Each fortification was well supplied with artillery and smaller gunpowder weapons, although heavy guns were very rare. Sustaining the frontier was a heavy financial burden for a rather small state such as the Transylvanian Principality. Local resources were insufficient, so central authorities had to resort to other sources of income in order to sustain the defensive system. The chain of defensive fortification constituted a complex institutional system, characterised by a specific social dynamic and marked by endemic warfare.

Hinterland Fiscal Fortifications

The Carpathian Mountains constituted a natural obstacle on the southern, eastern and northern borders of the Transylvanian Principality. There were no significant territorial changes in these areas and relations with neighbouring Moldavia and Wallachia were generally good. All three states were officially vassals of the Ottoman Empire and when they chose to oppose the sultan's authority they did so as allies.

---

49 *Călători străini*, vol. II, p.554.
50 Veress (ed.), *Documente*, vol. IV, pp.71–72.

Mounted Transylvanian noble and a conscripted peasant (second half of the sixteenth century)

(Illustration by Cătălin Drăghici © Helion & Company 2022)

See Colour Plate Commentaries for further information.

Mounted Székely *lófő* (early seventeenth century)
(Illustration by Cătălin Drăghici © Helion & Company 2022)
See Colour Plate Commentaries for further information.

Plate C

Saxon Black Guard from the town of Sibiu and a field cannon (second half of the sixteenth century)

(Illustration by Cătălin Drăghici © Helion & Company 2022)

See Colour Plate Commentaries for further information.

Guardsman (*drabant*) from the garrison of a western border fortification in Transylvania (second half of the sixteenth century)
(Illustration by Cătălin Drăghici © Helion & Company 2022)
See Colour Plate Commentaries for further information.

German *landesknecht* from the army of Giovanni Battista Castaldo (1551–1553)
(Illustration by Cătălin Drăghici © Helion & Company 2022)
See Colour Plate Commentaries for further information.

Spanish arquebusier from the army of Giovanni Battista Castaldo (1551–1553)

(Illustration by Cătălin Drăghici © Helion & Company 2022)

See Colour Plate Commentaries for further information.

Wallachian *curtean* from the army of Michael the Brave in Transylvania (1599–1600)

(Illustration by Cătălin Drăghici © Helion & Company 2022)

See Colour Plate Commentaries for further information.

Silesian cuirassier in the army of Giorgio Basta (early seventeenth century)
(Illustration by Cătălin Drăghici © Helion & Company 2022)
See Colour Plate Commentaries for further information.

Transylvanian rulers had strong fortifications in most regions of the country. They served as residencies of the ruling family and offered shelter in case of foreign invasions. The villages and towns situated on their estates were an important source of income and provided soldiers for the Transylvanian army. Later, in the second half of the seventeenth century, after the Turks conquered Oradea in 1660, some of the hinterland fortifications became part of a new military border.

Deva

Built on a high ridge along the Mureş valley, Deva was the most important fiscal fortification in Hunedoara County. The medieval fiscal fortress was first mentioned in an official document in 1265. Transylvanian voivodes administered the fortress until the second half of the fourteenth century.[51] During the second half of the sixteenth century, the fortress and its estate, consisting of two market towns and 38 villages, were under the direct authority of Transylvanian rulers. In 1553, the fortress was defended by a permanent garrison of 20 cavalry and 20 infantry.[52] The captaincy of Deva fortress was considered an important military office and was entrusted to leading members of the Transylvania nobility. Geszthi Ferenc held this position during the first phase of the Long Turkish War (1591–1606), while he was also appointed captain general of the Transylvanian army. His main responsibility was to coordinate military operations along the Mureş valley and in the Banat area.[53] In 1601 the fortress and its consistent estate were donated to Borbély György, an influential noble and renowned military commander.[54]

Alba Iulia

Further east, along the Mureş valley, Alba Iulia became the favourite residence of Transylvanian rulers in the second half of the sixteenth century. During the Middle Ages, Alba Iulia was the seat of the Transylvanian bishop. A fortification was built upon an ancient Roman *castrum*, to protect the cathedral, the chapter house and the bishop's residence. In 1542 the large estate of the bishopric was secularised and soon after, Queen Isabella Jagiellon moved into the bishop's palace. While Transylvania was under Habsburg rule (1551–1556), a new fortification was constructed in Alba Iulia. It was a rectangular enceinte with four bastions. The work stagnated after Castaldo and his army retreated from Transylvania (1553) and was resumed more than half a century later in 1614, under Prince Gabriel Bethlen.[55]

The Habsburgs also organised the first modern arsenals in Transylvania. The main one was established in Sibiu, but a smaller arsenal was also organised

---

51 Rusu, *Castelarea carpatică*, p.516.

52 Veress, *Arcélek Erdély*, f. 71.

53 Zsolt Trócsányi, *Erdély központi kormányzata. 1540–1690* (Budapest: Akadémiai Kiadó, 1980), pp.337–338; Ardelean, 'Military leadership', p.347.

54 Veress (ed.), *Documente*, vol. VI, p.370.

55 András Kovács, 'Gyulafehérvár, site of the Transylvanian princely court in the sixteenth century', Gyöngy Kovács Kiss (ed.), *Studies in the History of early modern Transylvania* (New York: Columbia University Press, 2011), pp.320–322.

in Alba Iulia.[56] The activity of the arsenal from Alba Iulia increased after 1556 and became the main site for weapons production. Local and foreign craftsmen were employed by Transylvanian rulers during the second half of the sixteenth century. In 1564, Damianus Leppler (*praefectus armamentarii*) arrived in Alba Iulia from Hungary. His activity within the arsenal was much appreciated by the John Sigismund Szapolyai who offered him a patent of nobility in 1568. Albert Almási, Hieronimus Vitalis Cremonensis (*capitaneus armamentarii*), Themistocles Venustus and Giovanni Fiotta (*capitaneus armamentarii*) worked in the arsenal of Alba Iulia and commanded the artillery of the Transylvanian army during the reign of Sigismund Báthory. One of the largest pieces of artillery forged in the foundry of Alba Iulia was the so-called Wolf (*Farkas*) Cannon, able to fire a 50-pound (28kg) cannonball. The cannon was made by Mauritius Hass of Salzburg and a goldsmith from Sighişoara, Jeremias Aurifaber. It became a symbol of princely authority in Transylvania and was displayed and used on ceremonial occasions.[57]

Făgăraş

The fortress and district (*ţara*) of Făgăraş were situated between the Olt River and the southern range of the Carpathians. The region maintained a specific juridical status within the Principality of Transylvania and was home to the boyars of Făgăraş, representatives of the local Romanian social elite. The fortification was probably built during the fifteenth century and was gradually improved throughout the sixteenth century.[58] After the battle of Mohács (1526), the fortress and its estate were given to Stephen Mailat, a descendant of a local boyar family. Mailat became one of the most powerful Transylvanian nobles and was able to maintain his position by repeatedly switching allegiance between Ferdinand of Habsburg and John Szapolyai. In 1540, after he was besieged for several months in the fortress of Făgăraş, Mailat was captured by the Turks.[59] While Bishop Martinuzzi ruled Transylvania (1541–1552) he also kept direct control over Făgăraş fortress. In 1563, John Sigismund Szapolyai bought the fortress and its estate from the Mailat family and thus Făgăraş became a part of the fiscal estate.[60] Later, the fortress and its large estate (60 settlements) were given to various high-ranking nobles for their faithful service, such as Gaspar Bekes, Balthazar Báthory and Stephan Csáky.[61]

Gherla

George Martinuzzi began the construction of a new residence and fortification at Gherla, on the right bank of the Someş River, in 1538. The plan of the fortress, an irregular quadrilateral with four bastions and one semi-bastion, was elaborated by an Italian architect, Domenico da Bologna. Stone

---

56 Cîmpeanu, 'The Royal Habsburg Arsenal', p.263.
57 Kovács, 'Gyulafehérvár', pp.323–326.
58 Antal Lukács, *Ţara Făgăraşului în Evul Mediu (secolele XIII–XVI)* (Bucureşti: Editura Enciclopedică, 1999), pp.116–117.
59 Ioan-Aurel Pop, 'Ştefan Mailat şi ţara (cu cetatea) Făgăraşului', *Mediaevalia Transilvanica*, II:2 (1998), pp.239–244.
60 *Chronicon Fuchsio-Lupino-Oltardinum*, vol. I, p.64.
61 Veress (ed.), *Documente*, vol. III, pp.158–163; vol. VI, pp.375–379.

was the main construction material. After the assassination of Martinuzzi in December 1551, Castaldo took direct control of the fortress. In 1553 it became the residence of one of the newly appointed voivodes, István Dobó. Gherla was protected by a permanent garrison of 60–70 soldiers at the time. The defending force was increased by the personal retinue of Dobó (330 horsemen) and other soldiers from the estate of the fortress. In 1556, Gherla remained the last fortification under Habsburg rule in Transylvania. István Dobó and his troops were able to defend the fortress for 10 months before they willingly surrendered. In the following decades, the fortress remained a part of the fiscal estate and was considered one of the safest fortifications inside the country. The treasury and also the princely family often resided within its walls.[62] The importance of this hinterland princely fortress is also illustrated by the size of its estate. In 1553 it consisted of one market town and 22 villages[63] and in 1607 it was expanded to 74 settlements, with 586 serf families.[64] The conscription record and inventory made in 1607 also mentions 48 guns of various calibres and a significant number of firearms.[65]

Gurghiu

Gurghiu was among the medieval fortifications of Transylvania which benefited from an extensive period of modernisation during the sixteenth and seventeenth centuries. First mentioned by a document issued in 1364, Ghurgiu was a fiscal fortress, situated in the vicinity of the Eastern Carpathians. It was an important border fortification and seat of the Count of the Székelys.[66] The first bastions were probably built during the years 1553–1556 by Antonio da Bufalo, an Italian architect in the service of the Habsburgs.[67] By 1640 the fortress had three bastions and the construction of a fourth was about to begin.[68]

In the second half of the sixteenth century the fortress and its surrounding settlements were integrated into the fiscal estate. The infantry garrison of Gurghiu was responsible for maintaining public order in the surrounding area. Most garrisons of hinterland fortifications played a similar role. Fortresses also fulfilled the role of prisons. In 1594, the Transylvanian Diet delegated this authority to several fortress captains and their soldiers. The garrisons of Gurghiu and Brâncovenești (Vécs) acted in Cluj and Turda counties, the garrisons from Beclean and Gherla maintained order in Inner Szolnok and Dăbâca counties, while the garrison of Făgăraș had jurisdiction over Alba and Târnave counties.[69]

62 Klára Kovács, *Cetatea din Gherla. Răspândirea fortificației în sistem bastionar italian în Transilvani*a (PhD Thesis) (Cluj-Napoca: Babeș-Bolyai University, 2009), pp.42–57.

63 Prodan, *Iobăgia*, vol. I, p.136.

64 Gheorghe Sebestyén, 'Cronologia cetății Gherla (II)', *Studii și Materiale de Istorie Medie*, XVII (1999), p.227.

65 Kovács, *Cetatea din Gherla*, p.59.

66 Liviu Ursuțiu, *Domeniul Ghurghiu (1652–1706): Urbarii inventare și socoteli economice* (Cluj-Napoca: Editura Argonaut, 2007), p.5.

67 Kovács, *Cetatea din Gherla*, p.205.

68 *Memorialul lui Nagy Szabó Ferencz*, pp.198–199.

69 *MCRT*, vol. III, pp.461–462.

Odorheiu Secuiesc and Leţ-Várhegy

After defeating the Székely rebellion in 1562, John Sigismund Szapolyai decided to build two fortifications within their territories. This was against the traditional privileges of their community but was considered a necessary measure, meant to increase the control of the central authorities over this troublesome community. The two fortresses had meaningful symbolic names: Odorheiu Secuiesc (*Székelytámadt* – the Székely attacks) and Leţ-Várhegy (*Székelybánja* – the Székely repents). Both were modern fortifications with angular bastions. Leţ-Várhegy was destroyed in 1599 when Michael the Brave restored the privileges of the Székely community. Odorheiu Secuiesc survived until the beginning of the eighteenth century.[70]

The fiscal estate was an important source of income for Transylvanian rulers. The prince was thus the most important landowner in the country although in theory he shared authority over these lands with the Diet. Most of these estates were concentrated around fortifications. Hinterland fiscal fortifications share many similarities with those from the Western border. Most of them were improved according to modern military architecture principles and were defended by permanent mercenary garrisons and semi-privileged groups of soldiers living in the nearby villages.

Fortified Towns

Some of the most developed urban settlements in early modern Transylvania were situated on the lands of the Saxon University. Hungarian kings granted several privileges to Saxon communities in the eastern parts of their kingdom, including the right to erect stone walls around their towns. The building of defensive fortifications was intensified in the beginning of the fourteenth century, due to the increasing Ottoman threat. Sibiu, Braşov, Mediaş, Bistriţa, Sighişoara, Sebeş and other Saxon towns invested local resources in the building of defensive walls and towers.

Braşov

The town of Braşov was attacked and pillaged by an Ottoman raiding party in 1421 because the enceinte was not finished at the time. Later, in 1432 and 1438, the citizens of Braşov took cover behind their defensive walls and successfully resisted Ottoman attacks. By the end of the fifteenth century, Braşov was defended by three kilometres of stone wall, 1.70–2.20 metres thick with a median height of 12 metres. At regular intervals the wall was defended by 32 rectangular towers, well provisioned with weapons and artillery.[71] Complex military regulations, containing 24 articles, were issued by town authorities in 1491. They established the organisation of the town

---

70 Kovács, *Cetatea din Gherla*, pp.124–125.

71 Liviu Cîmpeanu, 'Organizarea militară a Braşovului până la sfârşitul secolului al XV-lea', Vasile Ciobanu, Dan Dumitru Iacob (eds), *Studii de istorie a oraşelor: in honorem Paul Niedermaier* (Bucureşti: Editura Academiei Române; Brăila: Editura Istros a Muzeului Brăilei "Carol I", 2017, pp.337–343.

militia, the distribution of troops along the defensive perimeter, the chain of command and the use of flags and acoustic signals during sieges.[72] In 1524, the inhabitants of Brașov began building a new fortification, a citadel situated close to the town. The construction of the citadel advanced under the supervision of Count Felix de Arco, a colonel in the Habsburg army of General Castaldo. A large ditch and an earth rampart were added in 1611.[73]

Sibiu

Sibiu was first fortified in the thirteenth century, in response to the Great Mongol Invasion (1241). Two distinct defensive walls were built during this period. Towards the end of the Middle Ages, Sibiu became an important trading and manufacturing centre and the town extended beyond the original defensive walls. A new enceinte was built in the sixteenth century following the most recent developments in military architecture.[74] The new fortifications of Sibiu were supervised by Italian architects brought to Transylvania during the Habsburg rule of 1551–1556. The first bastion (the so-called Haller bastion) was built during this period. Three more were constructed during the reigns of John Sigismund Szapolyai, Stephen Báthory and Sigismund Báthory. The finalisation of all four bastions required both local resources and subsidies provided by central authorities.[75]

At the end of the Middle Ages, Sibiu was the most important Transylvanian centre of military equipment production. Several guilds and craftsmen from this town produced bows, crossbows, shields, armour, various types of pole arms and guns.[76] According to local accounts, at least 48 citizens from Sibiu were involved in weapon manufacturing in the second half of the fifteenth century and the beginning of the sixteenth century. The weapons produced here were destined for local needs but also for trade beyond the Carpathians, in Moldavia and Wallachia.[77] Thus, it was no mere coincidence that in 1551 General Castaldo decided to establish the main arsenal of the Habsburg army sent to Transylvania in Sibiu. In February 1552, Conrad Haas was named commander (*zeugwart*) of the arsenal. His main task was to supply the Habsburg troops in Transylvania and the Banat with weapons and other war material. His staff consisted of craftsmen (coopers, carpenters, locksmiths, blacksmiths, wheelwrights etc.), gunners and sentinels. In this early phase, the arsenal functioned mainly as a space for storage and maintenance and only occasionally to produce new weapons. The army of Castaldo arrived in Transylvania well supplied with weapons and ammunition and in the following years new transports were dispatched from Upper Hungary.[78] An

---

72 Cîmpeanu, 'Organizarea militară', pp.357–359.
73 Kovács, *Cetatea din Gherla*, pp.108–109.
74 Mária Pakucs-Willcocks, *Sibiul veacului al XVI-lea: rânduirea unui oraș transilvănean* (București: Humanitas, 2018), p.157.
75 Kovács, *Cetatea din Gherla*, pp.102–104.
76 Ioan Marian Țiplic, *Bresle și arme în Transilvania (secolele XVI–XVI)* (București: Editura Militară, 2009), pp.59–128.
77 Szabolcs László Kozák-Kígyóssy, 'Fegyverkészítő kézműiparosok és céhek a késő középkori Nagyszebenben', *Hadtörténelmi Közlemények* 3 (2018), pp.539–560.
78 Cîmpeanu, 'The Royal Habsburg Arsenal', pp.258–261.

The town of Cluj and its surroundings at the beginning of the seventeenth century, illustrated by Georg Hoefnagel, 1617. (The National Museum of Transylvanian History, Cluj-Napoca, Romania)

inventory drafted by Conrad Haas in 1551 mentions 45 cannons, two mortars, 186 double arquebuses, 1,327 regular arquebuses and handguns and 5,191 pikes.[79] These weapons were stored in the arsenal of Sibiu but, between 1552 and 1555, significant quantities of weapons, ammunition and construction material were sent to various locations throughout Transylvania. In 1568 the arsenal was entrusted to the magistrate of Sibiu.

Cluj

Although the medieval town of Cluj (*Klausenburg*) was founded by Saxon settlers it was not included in the lands of the Saxon University. Cluj was positioned in the centre of Transylvania, on the main trade routes that linked this region to Central Europe. Commerce and crafts were the main economic activities. Cluj became a 'free city' in 1316 and soon after, the construction of a defensive wall began.[80] A new privilege, which explicitly mentions the right to build stone walls and towers, was issued by King Sigismund of Luxemburg in 1405.[81] The building of the defensive enceinte was a long process that lasted until the beginning of the sixteenth century. Additional elements of defence were also constructed during the sixteenth and seventeenth centuries.[82] The crafting guilds were initially responsible for repairing, supplying and

79 Paul Abrudan, Fritz Sontag, 'Sistemul de apărare al cetății Sibiului în secolele XV și XVI– expresie a concepției războiului popular', *Studii și Materiale de Muzeografie și Istorie Militară*, 7–8 (1974–1975), p.129.

80 Rusu, *Castelarea*, p.512.

81 Samuel Goldenberg, *Clujul în sec. XVI: Producția și schimbul de mărfuri* (Cluj: Editura Academiei Republicii Populare Române, 1958), pp.111–112.

82 András Kovács, *Késő reneszánsz építészet Erdélyben. 1541–1720* (Budapest–Kolozsvár: Teleki László Alapítvány, Polis Könyvkiadó, 2003), p.200.

defending the towers and walls of Cluj.[83] In the second half of the sixteenth century, the task of defending the town was entrusted to a mercenary garrison. In 1576, Stephen Báthory allowed the citizens of Cluj to retain 213 florins from their due taxes for the payment of the infantry garrison.[84] The size of the defensive force was usually increased during times of war. In 1601, for example, 300 soldiers were taken into service, but they were unable to defend the town from the Habsburg troops led by General Giorgio Basta.[85]

The fortifications of major urban settlements were meant to protect the citizens living within. In most cases, the stone walls and towers were built during the fourteenth and fifteenth centuries and improved over the course of the sixteenth and seventeenth centuries. The cost of building and repairing these fortifications was supported by the local community but central authorities often contributed with tax exemptions and sometimes even with subsidies. The defensive forces were initially recruited among the local population but during the sixteenth century these was gradually replaced by mercenary troops. Transylvanian towns were usually well supplied with weapons and gunpowder. Most towns had at least a few crafting guilds who produced weapons for local needs, while towns like Sibiu were able to supply the whole region and even trade weapons beyond Transylvanian borders.

Fortified Churches

Building fortifications around churches and monasteries was a common practice throughout medieval Europe. The Kingdom of Hungary and Transylvania made no exception. Initially, these walls did not have a military purpose. They were meant to define the sacred space of the church and protect the Holy Sacraments.[86] In Transylvania, most fortified churches were located in the southern parts of the region and were built by Saxon communities. The oldest were built during the thirteenth century but many of them were modified and improved during the fifteenth and sixteenth centuries. Prosperous Saxon rural communities could afford to build modern fortifications supplied with gunpowder weapons. The Ottoman threat and the political instability that affected Transylvania during the late Middle Ages changed the initial purpose of fortified churches. They became a place of refuge for the local community. Even during the eighteenth century, fortified churches were used to store valuable items and food.[87]

---

83 Goldenberg, *Clujul*, p.212.
84 Veress (ed.), *Báthory István*, vol. II, p.18.
85 Crăciun, *Cronicarul Szamosközy*, p.154.
86 Rusu, *Castelarea*, p.456.
87 Hermann Fabini, *Universul cetăților bisericești din Transilvania* (Sibiu: Editura Monumenta, 2009), pp.58–78.

4

Military Campaigns, Battles and Sieges

Transylvania had a role to play in all major confrontations between the Ottomans and the Habsburgs in central and south-east Europe. Although they were officially vassals of the Turkish sultan, Transylvanian rulers occasionally sided with the emperors from Vienna and Prague. Their military potential and strategic position was considered strong enough to upset the balance of power between the two great empires. Regardless of their political orientation, all Transylvanian rulers from this period (1541–1613) were concerned with maintaining autonomy and expanding their rule over the highly disputed western borderland, where most battles were fought. Sometimes, foreign invading armies or local opposing factions brought the devastating effects of war into the country. External military interventions were organised in Upper Hungary, Wallachia and Moldavia.

The Army of General Castaldo in Transylvania (1551–1553)

In 1526, after the death of King Louis II, Ferdinand of Habsburg claimed the Hungarian Crown for himself. Although he only managed to take control over the northern and western regions of the kingdom, Ferdinand's intention was to rule over all the lands of the Hungarian Crown. Following this political plan he and his successors tried to take Transylvania through diplomatic and military means. A first attempt was made in 1551 after months of negotiations with Queen Isabella Jagiellon and Bishop Martinuzzi. A small army of mercenaries under the command of Count Giovanni Battista Castaldo was sent to Transylvania. Its task was to support the new administration and to protect the newly acquired territories from Turkish attacks. Castaldo was an Italian nobleman who had served in the armies of Charles V. He took part in some of the most important confrontations with the French in Northern Italy like Bicocca (1522) and Pavia (1525). By the time he was entrusted with the leadership of the Transylvanian expeditionary force, he was considered an accomplished military commander.[1]

As soon as Ferdinand reached an agreement with George Martinuzzi, Habsburg troops were dispatched in the border area. A small vanguard of 475 hussars crossed the Tisa River at the beginning of May 1551. Two hundred were sent to reinforce the garrison of Făgăraș while the rest joined the retinue of the Transylvanian treasurer.[2] Swift military intervention was necessary because Queen Isabella had changed her mind and refused to give up Transylvania without a fight. She had some of the Transylvanian nobles on her side but an Ottoman intervention in her favour was considered a far greater danger. In the meantime, Giovanni Battista Castaldo, Count of Piadena and Marquis of Cassano, had arrived at the Viennese court. Here he spent a few days in the company of the Emperor and of Archduke Maximilian. On 1 May 1551 he headed for the fortress of Eger where most of his troops were concentrated. He travelled slowly and made a few stops on his way because he was asked to inspect the fortresses of Győr and Komárom.[3] On 26 May, the small Habsburg army began marching towards Transylvania. The 7,400 soldiers (5,700 infantry and 1,700 cavalry) were recruited from various parts of the Habsburg Empire. The vanguard consisted of seven companies of Spanish infantry (1,200 men) under the command of Bernardo de Aldana, 500 Hungarian *hajdús*, 1,000 hussars and four light cannons. They were followed by a regiment of German infantry (3,000 men) lead by Count Felix de Arco, 300 mounted lancers and 100 cuirassiers. The German regiment had six pieces of light artillery attached. In the rearguard, 1,000 Hungarian infantry, 300 hussars and three light cannons protected the baggage train of the army.[4] The Habsburg army approached Transylvania from the north-west. They were able to cross the Western Carpathians without major opposition. A small detachment was left to besiege the castle of Almaș, where a group of nobles, loyal to the Queen, took refuge. Castaldo and most of his troops joined Bishop Martinuzzi who was besieging the town of Sebeș. Unable to gather her supporters or to ask for Turkish help, Queen Isabella surrendered after 20 days of siege and accepted the conditions offered by the Habsburgs.[5] Castaldo was able to take control of Transylvania without much effort because Habsburg diplomacy had already prepared this conquest. Martinuzzi made sure that most of the country would accept the new rule. A few skirmishes with isolated groups of discontented nobles and two short sieges were enough to extend Habsburg control beyond the Western Carpathians. Nevertheless, the internal situation was far from being stable. Queen Isabella and her infant son left the country but never gave up on their right to rule. Soon after the Habsburg soldiers had settled in their new quarters, quarrels and conflicts with the local population began. Hostility towards the new administration increased and many Transylvanians favoured a return to autonomy under Turkish suzerainty.

1   Mariano D'Ayala, 'Vita din Giambattista Castaldo famosissimo guerriero del secolo XVI', *Archivio Storico Italiano*, V:I (Firenze, 1867), pp.86–124.
2   Florin Nicolae Ardelean, 'Mercenarii străini și inovațiile militare moderne timpurii în Europa Central-Răsăriteană. Armata lui Castaldo în Transilvania și Banat', Banatica 25 (2015), p.41.
3   ÖStA, HHStA, Hungarica AA, Fas. 57, Konv. B, f. 152.
4   Centorio, *Comentarii*, pp.59–65.
5   Ferencz Ghymesi Forgách, *Magyar Historiaja: 1540–1572*, Fidél Majer (ed.), *Monumenta Hungariae Historica, Scriptores*, vol. XVI (Pest, 1866), p.12.

Giovanni Battista Castaldo (1493–1563), commander of the Habsburg army in Transylvania (1551–1553)

The greatest threat to the Habsburg rule in Transylvania was Ottoman military intervention. Castaldo was well aware of this and prepared as best as he could under the circumstances. The most exposed region to a Turkish attack was the Banat. István Losonci, a loyal Hungarian noble from the region, was entrusted with the preparations for its defence. With a large retinue of 1,000 cavalry he was able to take some of the smaller Turkish fortifications in the borderlands. Timişoara, the largest and best fortified settlement in the area was controlled by Peter Petrovic, an influential nobleman of South Slavic origin. Habsburg diplomacy was employed once more and Petrovic agreed to surrender Timişoara and all his other fortifications in the Banat in exchange for proprieties in Upper Hungary. In the meantime, Emperor Ferdinand dispatched new troops to Transylvania, including artillery and the military architects Alessandro da Urbino and Sigismondo Prato Vecchio.[6]

In August 1551, Bernardo de Aldana and his company of Spanish infantry were sent to reinforce the garrison of Timişoara. Several reports drafted during the following month mention the transportation of weapons, gunpowder and construction materials sent to Timişoara. On 6 September Aloisio Ordogna and his company of Spanish infantry accompanied a convoy consisting of three falconets, 140 barrels of gunpowder and 200 long pikes (*cuspides*). Most of the journey was made on small boats and rafts on the Mureş River.[7]

An Ottoman army, commanded by Mehmet Sokollu, the Beylerbey of Rumelia, gathered on the right bank of the Danube, near the settlement of Szalankemen (today Stari Salankamen in Serbia). The Turkish commander managed to mobilise an impressive force of about 16,000 soldiers. The Ottomans advanced with caution and spent precious time capturing several smaller fortifications in the area. Manned by small garrisons these fortresses were unable to resist the larger Ottoman force, and often surrendered without a fight. Nevertheless they achieved their strategic purpose, and the enemy army was delayed from reaching its main objective. Lipova was also conquered during this campaign, but the Ottomans had to leave behind a significant force to defend it. When they finally arrived at Timişoara during the second half of October, a cold and rainy autumn was already setting in.[8] Timişoara was a modern fortification defended by semi-circular bastions and surrounded by marshy terrain. A large garrison of 3,570 soldiers (2,020

---

6   Ardelean, 'Mercenarii străini', pp.43–44.
7   ÖStA, HHStA, Hungarica AA, Fas. 59, Konv. B, f. 44–45.
8   Forgách, *Magyar Historiaja*, pp.15–18.

cavalry and 1,550 infantry) was behind its wooden walls.[9] The Ottoman army was unable to encircle the fortress because the surrounding waters were swelled by heavy rain. They also lacked heavy artillery and were unable to breach the walls. Leading light cavalry detachments Losonci made daily attacks on the Ottoman camp. Although the defenders held the upper hand, the Turkish commander organised a general assault at the beginning of November. The Ottomans were unable to scale the walls and suffered many casualties in their attempt to take control of the main wooden bridge. Thus, after a futile siege of 20 days, the Rumelian beylerbey decided to retreat. Losonci's cavalry followed the retreating army and managed to retake most of the smaller fortifications lost at the beginning of the campaign.[10] In a report drafted on 9 November 1551, General Castaldo wrote that the Turks had lost over 3,000 men during this siege. Casualties among the defenders were less but the Spanish Captain Aloisio Ordogna lost his life together with most of his company. The remaining 40 soldiers were integrated into another Spanish detachment.[11]

Although the main Ottoman force had retreated south of the Danube, a considerable garrison of about 5,000 soldiers was left to defend Lipova. Castaldo and Martinuzzi agreed that such an important strategic point could not be left in the hands of the Turks. During the second half of November, a large army gathered in the vicinity of this disputed fortress. According to contemporary sources it numbered about 80,000 men.[12] Although this was undoubtedly an exaggeration it was nevertheless a massive concentration of troops that included most of the troops brought by Castaldo into Transylvania, noble levy and militias from several counties in Upper Hungary, Serbian mercenaries and the large retinue of Bishop Martinuzzi. In addition, the Transylvanian army, with the contingents provided by the nobility, the Saxons and the Székely, also reached the camp of the besiegers.[13] In spite of a huge numerical advantage, the Christian army did not dare to attempt an assault. Instead they prepared for a long siege by digging trenches and building artillery platforms. The besieging army was affected by the cold weather and the lack of provisions. Numerical superiority was becoming a serious disadvantage. Under these circumstances Martinuzzi proposed negotiations with the enemy force. Castaldo and the other Habsburg officers agreed, but later they accused the bishop of betrayal.[14] Eventually the Turkish garrison was persuaded to leave the fortress. Although they had received assurances regarding their lives and possessions, a group of Hungarian nobles and their soldiers attacked the former Ottoman garrison on its way to Belgrade. By the end of 1551 the Banat region was almost entirely under Habsburg control. Most irregular troops were disbanded and some of the

---

9   Czimer, 'Temesvár megvétele', I, pp.34.
10 Forgách, *Magyar Historiaja*, pp.19–22.
11 ÖStA, HHStA, Hungarica AA, Fas. 60, Konv. B, 22–23.
12 Centorio, *Comentarii*, p.108.
13 Cristina Feneşan, 'Codex Vindobonensis Palatinus 7803, eine wenig bekannte quelle über die eroberung von Lipova durch die Habsburger (1551)', *Revue des Études Sud-Est Européennes*, XVIII:1 (1980),pp.14–25.
14 Papo, Nemeth Papo, *Frate Giorgio Martinuzzi*, pp.310–311.

mercenaries were sent to reinforce local garrisons. A large detachment of 1,400 soldiers was quartered in Timișoara.[15]

During the first months of 1552 troubling news of an imminent Ottoman attack reached the Habsburg officials in Transylvania. The sultan was still focused on his war with Persia, but he had enough resources to organise a more effective campaign than the previous one against his European rival. This time attacks were also expected from Moldavia and Wallachia and Castaldo decided to send some of his troops to the southern and eastern border of Transylvania. Smaller or larger groups of Habsburg soldiers were scattered throughout the province. The paymaster had a hard time reaching them all and his funds were in any case insufficient. Unpaid wages generated a wave of discontent among the Spanish, German and Hungarian mercenaries. Their first reaction was to pillage the countryside further increasing the hostility of Transylvanians towards the Habsburg administration. In a report sent to Emperor Ferdinand in April 1552, Castaldo estimated that an additional sum of 60,000 florins was necessary to pay the wages of his soldiers.[16]

In 1552, the Ottoman campaign in the Banat was logistically and strategically much better prepared. The attacks from Moldavia and Wallachia prevented a massive concentration of Habsburg troops in the Banat. For the same reason, the Transylvanian estates refused to send their contingents away from home. Kara Ahmed, the newly appointed Ottoman commander, was able to gather a large army and 36 siege guns (*tormentis muralibus*).[17] The Ottoman army began the campaign earlier and on 27 June it reached the walls of Timișoara. The summer was hot and dry and the waters that surrounded the fortress were at a very low level, no longer an obstruction to the besieging army. The garrison consisted of approximately 2,500 soldiers, considerably smaller when compared to the 3,570 from the previous year. Nevertheless, Stephen Losonci was not willing to give up his stronghold without a fight. His troops were of various origins; local soldiers accustomed to border warfare and foreign Habsburg mercenaries. Among them were the Spaniard, Captain Alonso Perez with 200 Hungarian cavalry, Gaspar Castelvi from Sardinia with 300 Spanish foot, 300 infantry from Bohemia, 100 German infantry and some Hungarian nobles with their mounted retinues (Perényi with 100 cavalry, Serédi with 100 cavalry and Simon Forgách with 60 cavalry). Proceeding with caution, Kara Ahmed encircled the fortress and maintained an efficient blockade for an entire month. He also made good use of his superior siege artillery causing serious damage to various sections of the wall. The turning point of this siege was the capture of the so-called 'water tower', an advanced bastion that defended the main gateway into the fortress. On day 32 of the siege, the Ottoman commander (*serdar*) ordered a general assault focused on the 'water tower', defended by the Spanish detachment. Unable to resist the overwhelming number of Ottoman soldiers the Spanish were defeated and their captain, Castelvi, was killed in battle.[18]

---

15 ÖStA, HHSta, Hungarica AA, Fas. 61, Konv. Konv. C, 21.
16 Ardelean, 'Mercenarii străini', pp.49–50.
17 Bethlen, *Historia*, vol. I, pp.540–541.
18 Forgách, *Magyar Historiaja*, pp.37–38.

Losing hope of any help from outside, Losonci and his officers decided to give up the fortress. As was the custom they negotiated their surrender and received assurances that their lives were in no danger. While the defeated army was leaving the fortress an incident occurred and Losonci was attacked by Turkish soldiers. He lost his life in the skirmish together with many of his companions. According to the Ottoman chronicler Mustafa Gelalzade, the attack was caused by the fact that Losonci broke the agreement and was taking valuable goods and prisoners from the fortress.[19] Other sources claimed that the Turks were taking revenge for the similar treatment received by the Ottoman garrison of Lipova in the winter of 1551.

When news of the fall of Timișoara reached Lipova, Bernardo de Aldana, commander of the garrison, decided to flee. Later he was accused of treason and imprisoned for a while in Hungary.[20] Without facing any major opposition, the Ottomans were able to occupy most of the Banat region and some fortifications situated north of the Mureș valley. A large part of the conquered territory was organised as a new Ottoman province, the *vilayet* of Timișoara.[21]

The state of Habsburg rule in Transylvania had reached a critical point in 1553. A local rebellion threatened internal stability and another Ottoman attack was expected on the south-western section of the frontier. It was in this area, in the vicinity of Deva fortress, where most of the remaining Habsburg troops were concentrated. Castaldo managed to secure a loan of 3,200 florins from Cluj and paid the wages of his small army of 1,420 soldiers (720 cavalry and 700 infantry).[22] Soon after, the Habsburg Emperor decided to recall all foreign troops from Transylvania and General Castaldo resigned from his position of governor. Instead, two voivodes were appointed, Francis Kendi and Stephen Dobó. Without direct support from the Ottomans the rebels were scattered, and Transylvania remained under the nominal rule of the Habsburgs for three more years.

Although his soldiers were some the best in Christian Europe at the time (Spanish *tercios* and German *landesknechte*) Castaldo was unable to keep Transylvania under his control or stop the Ottoman conquest of the Banat. There were several reasons for these failures. First of all, his army was too small (only about 7,000 troops) for the vast territory it was supposed to keep under control. Cooperation with local military contingents was not always effective. Insufficient provisions and unpaid wages seriously affected the performance of the army and created a context for conflicts with the local population. The Transylvanian political elite were not fully committed to the Habsburg cause and many nobles remained loyal, openly or in secret, to the Szapolyai family. Considering all these issues the clear conclusion is that the campaign was a political and logistical failure rather than a military one. Nevertheless, this failed military and political project had some positive consequences for

---

19 Guboglu, Mehmet (eds), *Cronici turcești*, vol. I, p.286.
20 Zoltán Korpás, 'Lo que no figura en 'La Expedición': El motín del tercio viejo de Bernardo Aldana en Hungría, 1553', *Libros de la Corte* 21:12 (2020), pp.63–91.
21 Feneșan, *Vilayetul Timișoara*, pp.19–29.
22 Veress, *Arcélek Erdély*, f. 71.

Transylvania. The Habsburg troops, fighting alongside Transylvanian soldiers, contributed to the spread of new military knowledge and technology in these parts of Europe. The Habsburgs also came with a new model of military administration based on centralised decision making, with a large number of officers and a centralised supply of weapons and war materials stored in arsenals. One of the most visible effects of the Habsburg rule of 1551–1556 was the spread of the new type of bastioned fortifications which greatly enhanced the defensive potential of Transylvania.[23]

Transylvania and the Fortress Wars (1556–1570)

In 1556 Queen Isabella Jagiellon and her son, John Sigismund, returned to Transylvania. In preparation for their arrival, the Transylvanian Diet decided to expel all remaining Habsburg troops from the country. These events marked the beginning of a prolonged conflict between Transylvania and the Habsburg mMonarchy that was concluded by the Treaty of Speyer in 1570. Habsburg–Transylvanian hostilities coincided roughly with the so-called 'Fortress Wars' (1557–1568) fought between the Habsburgs and the Ottomans in Northern Hungary.[24] During these years Transylvania acted as a faithful vassal of the Ottoman Empire. Transylvanian and Turkish troops often fought together against the common enemy although their immediate strategic goals were sometimes very different. The heir of House Szapolyai fought this war to regain disputed territories in Upper Hungary and north-west Transylvania. Most campaigns took place in these regions and their objective was the conquest of important fortifications from the borderlands.

In 1556 the representatives of the Transylvanian estates entrusted the leadership of their troops to Peter Petrovic, an experienced military commander, and one faithful to the Szapolyai family. The Turkish sultan had also decided to support his Transylvanian vassals and ordered the rulers of Moldavia and Wallachia to send troops to their aid. Most pro-Habsburg Transylvanians fled or pledged their allegiance to the new ruler with one notable exception. Stephen Dobó, one of the voivodes appointed by the Habsburgs in 1553, decided to resist behind the walls of Gherla fortress. Local troops and Moldavian soldiers were dispatched to begin the siege of this important fortification. Petrovic asked the authorities of Sibiu to send 300 infantry (*pedites sclopetarios*) and siege artillery. Judge Johannes Roth agreed to send the required soldiers but refused to give up the artillery that was considered essential for the defence of the town.[25] Soon after, Sibiu was engulfed in a devastating fire followed by a riot and the murder of the royal judge. These incidents showed that the allegiance of the Saxons was still divided and Petrovic himself had to restore order in Sibiu.[26] Meanwhile the

---

23   Ardelean, 'Foreign mercenaries', pp.124–125.
24   Pálffy, *The Kingdom of Hungary*, p.50.
25   Bethlen, *Historia*, vol. I, pp.585–586.
26   Pakucs-Willcocks, *Sibiul*, pp.107–121.

siege of Gherla continued, and the attacking army was unable to make any progress without sufficient siege artillery.

Through negations or force, Petrovic was gradually gathering the whole country under one banner. In June 1556, the Diet was summoned near Gherla, and met in the camp of the army. The siege was obviously the main topic of discussion. The representatives of the estates agreed to continue the siege and decided to dig a trench around the perimeter of the fortress in order to make the blockade more efficient.[27] Queen Isabella and her son reached the town of Cluj in October and thus it became clear that the Habsburg rule in Transylvania was over. Dobó himself realised that he was fighting for a lost cause and decided to surrender under certain conditions. Safe passage to Hungary was promised to him, his family and his retinue (about 300 soldiers) but when they arrived in Cluj, the Queen changed her mind and decided to imprison them. They were first detained in town and later sent back to Gherla, this time as prisoners. After almost one year of detention, Dobó and his remaining companions were allowed to return home.[28]

The significant length, almost nine months, of the siege/blockade of Gherla fortress in 1556 was determined by several factors. First of all, the recently constructed modern fortification, well supplied with gunpowder weapons and provisions, had great defensive potential. Stephen Dobó was one of the best Hungarian commanders at the time, having recently gained valuable experience and reputation as defender of Eger fortress in 1552. The besieging army lacked cohesion and determination. Petrovic, and his Moldavian and Wallachian allies, were scattered throughout Transylvania chasing out the remaining Habsburg troops. Without heavy siege artillery, the armies loyal to the Szapolyai family were unable to breach the walls of the fortress and a large-scale assault was considered too costly. The siege ended through negotiations but the winners, in this case Queen Isabella, broke the terms of the surrender when she ordered the imprisonment of the garrison. In the following years Isabella Jagiellon was able to consolidate her rule over Transylvania while her loyal supporters continued to fight against Habsburg troops in the western borderlands. The Queen died in 1559 and her son, John Sigismund, continued to govern the country on his own. His intentions were peaceful, and he even tried to establish a matrimonial alliance with the Habsburgs, alas without success.

Hostilities between the two states resumed in the beginning of 1562. The Habsburgs were able to gain the upper hand because Menyhért Balassa, one of the most powerful magnates in Upper Hungary, betrayed House Szapolyai and pledged his loyalty to Vienna. Previously, Balassa had occupied the position of captain general (*capitaneus supremus*) of the Transylvanian army and was richly rewarded by the late Queen Isabella.[29] His Transylvanian estates became strategic outposts of the Habsburgs. In such a situation was the castle of Hodod, in north-western Transylvania, commanded by György Suliok, a faithful retainer of Balassa. Retaking this fortification was the first

---

27 *MCRT*, vol. I, p.582.
28 *Quellen*, vol. IV, pp.519–520.
29 Ardelean, 'Military Leadership', p.345.

major objective set by John Sigismund and his councillors in the spring of 1562. The newly appointed captain general, Ferenc Németh, and the captain of Oradea fortress, Stephen Báthory, were sent to besiege the fortress. In response Balassa mobilised several nobles and Habsburg commanders from Upper Hungary with their retinues and marched towards the besieged castle. What began as a regular siege was about to turn into the most important pitched battle of this conflict.

The Transylvanian army consisted of about 8,000 soldiers, including Saxon infantry detachments, county nobles and their mounted retinues, soldiers from the garrison of Oradea (about 500 men) a detachment of court infantry armed with arquebuses under the command of László Radák, and several pieces of medium and light artillery. Németh and his troops occupied a high ground in the vicinity of Hodod castle.

The Habsburg force was significantly smaller. Balassa was able to gather only 4,000 men, but they were experienced Hungarian and German troops from the borderlands. Among those who followed him in battle were Ferenc Zay, captain general of Košice, Székely Antal captain of Kisvárda fortress and Simon Forgács. They also had 10 field guns of various sizes.

The Transylvanian army was positioned on a hilltop and began firing their artillery as soon as the enemy approached into range. The infantry, consisting mostly of Saxon troops, armed with firearms, was positioned in the centre. Both flanks were secured by cavalry detachments. The Captain General himself was in charge of the left flank while the captain of Oradea fortress, Stephen Báthory, commanded the right flank. Balassa took the initiative and assaulted the left flank of the Transylvanian army. The cavalry charge was led by Simon Forgács, and it was successful, and Németh was unable to hold his ground. The Saxon infantry was also routed by a strong cavalry charge lead by Ferenc Zay. Stephen Báthory and his men attempted a counter-attack but were unable to prevent the collapse of the central Transylvanian detachments. Moreover, the captain of Oradea fortress and future Polish-Lithuanian king was seriously injured in the melee and was forced to flee the battlefield.[30]

Thus, in a matter of hours, on 4 March 1562, the Transylvanian army suffered a decisive defeat in a direct confrontation with a smaller force. There are several factors that determined this outcome. First, the superior quality of Habsburg troops combined with the daring and efficient tactical approach of Ballasa was the main reason for the Transylvanian defeat. Ballassa knew his enemy very well and was able to take advantage of their weaknesses. Németh had also made a tactical mistake by taking up defensive positions with an army dominated by light and semi-heavy cavalry, best suited for swift actions and flanking manoeuvres. Several high-ranking Transylvanian nobles were captured and were forced to pay significant ransoms for their release. One further outcome was the start of bitter rivalry between Stephen Báthory and Menyhért Balassa.

---

30 Endre Veress, *A történetíró Báthory István király* (Cluj-Kolozsvár: Minerva, 1933), pp.32–33; Ödön Hegyi, 'Székely Antal tudósítása a Hadadi csatáról', *Történelmi Tár* (1990), pp.142–144; Forgách, *Magyar Historiaja*, pp.230–232; Mathias Miles, *Siebenbürgischer Würg-Engel* (Hermannstadt, 1670), pp.83–85.

The war was not going well for the young Transylvanian state. Confronted with a major Székely rebellion at home, John Sigismund signed a one-year armistice with the Habsburgs in April 1562. As soon as the agreement expired, Balassa once again attacked Transylvanian territory. Simon Pauer, captain of the Saxon infantry, was captured during a small skirmish with some hussars in Habsburg service.[31] Small scale raids were performed regularly in various regions of the Transylvanian western borderlands. Occasionally, each side organised larger expeditions, but still involving less than 10,000 troops, which were aimed at retaking the most important fortifications in the frontier area. Such an expedition was led by Stephen Báthory in October 1564. In just a few weeks, the new Transylvanian captain general was able to conquer several fortresses and towns in Upper Hungary. His most spectacular achievement was the conquest of Satu Mare. Báthory was able to take the fortress through a surprise night attack with the help of some bribed guards. At the time, Satu Mare was a personal estate and residence of Balassa. Although he was not inside the fortification, his wife and two children were there, and were taken captives by his rival. After these events Balassa was no longer a threat to Transylvania. He spent his last years trying to free his family through futile negotiations. Báthory liberated them from captivity only after Balassa died.[32]

The loss of Satu Mare fortress was not taken lightly by Habsburg authorities. As soon as the Transylvanian troops returned home, Lazarus Schwendi mounted a counter-offensive. With a small army of 7,000 experienced troops from the borderlands, the Habsburg general was able to retake all fortifications lost during the previous months. By the end of February 1565, the Habsburgs were also able to expand their conquest in Transylvania by taking the fortress of Chioar.[33] Once again, John Sigismund Szapolyai was forced to accept the territorial changes and signed a peace treaty with the Habsburgs on 13 March 1565.

Hostilities resumed in 1566 when the young Transylvanian ruler was called to arms by his liege lord, the Ottoman sultan. Süleyman the Magnificent had decided to personally lead a campaign into Hungary. John Sigismund and his councillors summoned the Diet and began the preparations for war. The Transylvanian estates gathered in Turda at the end of May. Christopher Hagymássy, an influential nobleman with many estates in the north-western section of the border with Habsburg Hungary, was appointed captain general. The contribution of each estate was also established on this occasion. The Saxons agreed to send 2,500 infantry and to pay a total contribution of 24,000 florins. The counties and the Székely Seats organised local musters and prepared their men. Soon after the Diet was concluded, John Sigismund travelled with a large retinue (about 700 men) to meet the Ottoman sultan who was marching towards Hungary. They met on 29 June, in the camp of the Ottoman army at Zemun (today part of the modern city of Belgrade). After the oaths of fealty were renewed, the Transylvanian ruler joined his

---

31 *Chronicon Fuchsio-Lupino-Oltardinum*, vol. I, p.64.
32 Nándor Virovecz, *Balassa Menyhárt élete és a kora újkori magyar politikai kultúra* (PhD Thesis) (Budapest: Eötvös Loránd University, 2017), p.127.
33 Lukinich, *Erdély területi változásai*, p.116.

army which was marching towards Bihor County. This expedition was no different from previous campaigns fought in this conflict. The Habsburg troops avoided large confrontations and the Transylvanians were able to take a few minor forts on their way to Tokaj. This important fortification was defended by a strong garrison. Hagymássy decided that a direct assault was too risky and settled for a blockade, hoping that the Turks would provide reinforcements. The siege lasted until 4 October, when the Transylvanians received unsettling news. The main Ottoman force suddenly retreated from the siege of Szighetvár and was heading home. The reason was the unexpected death of Süleyman the Magnificent. Sensing a radical shift in the balance of the conflict, the Transylvanians also decided to retreat. Lazarus Schwendi took advantage of this situation and launched a counter-offensive east of the Tisa River. His target was once again the Western Transylvanian borderland. The winter campaign of Schwendi was a success. From late October 1566, until February 1567 his troops were able to take several fortifications which had been previously under Transylvanian control. However, they were met with fierce resistance at the fortress of Hust. The captain of this fortification was none other than the Transylvanian captain general, Hagymássy, a loyal supporter of the Szapolyai family.[34]

The Transylvanian army was summoned once more in the spring of 1567. It was a much larger force than the one gathered in the previous year and General Schwendi was willing to negotiate a truce. John Sigismund refused and imprisoned the Habsburg emissary. This expedition lasted almost three months and the most important achievement of the Transylvanian army was the conquest of the town of Baia Mare and Chioar fortress, which had been lost to Habsburgs in 1565.[35]

The new Ottoman sultan, Selim II, signed a peace treaty with the Habsburg Emperor, Maximilian II, in 1568. John Sigismund did not have the resources or the willingness to continue the war on his own. He also reached an agreement with the Habsburgs at Speyer in 1570 and officially surrendered his claim on the title of 'elected king' of Hungary. The most important outcome of this treaty was the establishment of a more stable border between Transylvania and Habsburg Hungary. Most territorial changes were in favour of the Habsburgs, and beyond the Western Carpathians, John Sigismund kept only the counties of Bihor, Crasna, Middle Szolnok and Maramureş.[36]

The long Habsburg–Transylvanian war from 1556–1570 had an important role in sealing the partition of Transylvania from the Hungarian kingdom. It was a conflict dominated by irregular warfare. Raids and small skirmishes in the frontier area were the most common forms of fighting. When both sides were able to mobilise larger forces, they focused on taking fortifications. Smaller garrisons usually surrendered without much opposition while modern fortifications, well supplied with men and provisions, were able to resist prolonged sieges, like Tokaj defended by a Habsburg garrison in 1566, and Hust, defended by a Transylvanian garrison in 1567. The only significant

---

34 Ardelean, 'Pecunia nervus belli', pp.218–219.
35 *MCRT*, vol. II, pp.260–261.
36 Ardelean, *Organizarea militară*, pp.253–254.

pitched battle (Hodod, 4 March 1562) was lost by the Transylvanians, although they had numerical superiority. This was a war of attrition and the faction with the most resources (clearly the Habsburgs) was able to win in the end.

The Rivalry Between Stephen Báthory and Gaspar Bekes (1571–1575)

John Sigismund Szapolyai died in 1571, without leaving an heir to the Transylvanian throne. The Estates were thus able to apply the principle of 'free election' (*libera electio*) and chose the most suitable ruler from the ranks of the nobility, in this case Stephen Báthory. Most of the country was satisfied with this decision, except Gaspar Bekes and a few other nobles who supported him. Bekes was held in high regard at court during the reign of John Sigismund and was the main representative of Transylvania at the Speyer peace treaty. He used the occasion to establish connections with the Viennese court and secured the support of Maximilian II for his claim to the Transylvanian throne. Nevertheless, the sultan confirmed Báthory as voivode, and the Habsburgs were not ready to risk another war with the Ottomans at the time.

Bekes continued to plot against the elected ruler and managed to gain the support of the discontented Székelys, who were always ready to take up arms in exchange for the restoration of their traditional privileges. Bekes retreated from court in 1572 and settled on his most important estate, Făgăraş, on the southern border of the country. One year later, in 1573, the Transylvanian voivode finally decided deal with the rebel nobleman. The army sent against Bekes consisted mostly of troops from the court guard, and was commanded by György Bánffi de Losoncz, captain of cavalry, Johannes Sasa and Mihály Vadas, captains of the court infantry.[37] Soon after the siege began, Bekes decided to flee with a few of his retainers and sought refuge in the lands of the Habsburgs. After 19 days of resistance the garrison surrendered. Most of the soldiers who defended the fortress pledged their allegiance to the Transylvanian voivode and were kept in his service.[38]

In the following years Bekes prepared his return to Transylvania. He spent most of his time in Hungary and Poland recruiting mercenaries for his army.[39] In 1575 he assembled his troops in the vicinity of Košice, where representatives of the Hungarian estates were attending a session of the Diet. His small army consisted of about 4,000 men and included Polish mercenaries, Hungarian and German soldiers from the border area, nobles and their retinues from Upper Hungary and a large group of Transylvanian nobles who had joined his cause. It was a good army, with wages paid in advance, but they had insufficient artillery. From Košice they travelled to the Satu Mare fortress. After dispatching several letters to other Transylvanian nobles, trying to persuade them to join his army, Bekes crossed the mountains

---

37 Bethlen, *Historia*, vol. II, p.275.
38 Veress (ed.), *Documente*, vol. II, p.17; Bethlen, *Historia*, vol. II, pp.276–279.
39 Veress (ed.), *Documente*, vol. II, p.66.

into Transylvania. His troops advanced along the Someș River, towards the town of Dej. They continued their march southwards until they reached Turda, where the Transylvanian Diet was supposed to gather. When Báthory found out about Bekes' plans, he annulled the Diet and mustered his army near Alba Iulia. Bekes was counting on the Székelys joining his army, so he decided to move his troops into their territory. He followed the most obvious route along the Mureș River.[40]

Báthory was well aware of the fact that most of the Székelys were ready to join the usurper, so he decided to intercept Bekes before he could join his allies. The legitimate voivode was able to gather an army of 6,000 soldiers. Most of the county nobility was able to reach the camp near Alba Iulia before the march began. Among them were some of the most important military office holders of the country like Gaspar Kornis, captain of Hust fortress, Cristofer Hagymási with a retinue of 200 horsemen, the Bánffy brothers with 200 cavalry, 300 cavalry from the Székely seat of Arieș, the ban of Lugoj and Caransebeș with 200 infantry and 200 soldiers sent by the ruler of Wallachia, Alexandru II Mircea. The Saxon University contributed with a detachment of 1,000 men under the command of the royal judge Augustin Helwig. The position of captain general was entrusted to Ladislau Gyulafi.[41]

The two armies made contact near Iernut, an estate of the Kendi family, situated in the Mureș valley. They initially avoided a major confrontation and continued to march along the river. Báthory had an important advantage, as his field artillery was commanded by an experienced Italian master gunner, Raphael Cinna Florentinus. Through small skirmishes and sustained cannon fire, the Transylvanians were able to gain a moral and strategic advantage over their enemies. Eventually the two armies formed up opposite each other near the village of Sânpaul on 9 July 1575. Both commanders decided to mingle cavalry and infantry detachments on their flanks. The battle began in the morning and lasted until dusk. Báthory took the initiative and ordered his court infantry, known as the 'blue guardsmen', to attack. They were soon followed by a cavalry charge commanded by the captain general of the Transylvanian army, Ladislau Gyulafi. Both these attacks were directed towards the centre of Bekes' army and were repelled. The Transylvanian voivode himself led an attack on the right flank and the enemy army began to lose cohesion. Bekes decided, once again, that he had no chance of victory and fled the battlefield.[42]

This was an important military success for Báthory, which consolidated his authority in Transylvania and improved his reputation among neighbouring countries. His ability to defeat a pretender backed by the Habsburgs impressed the Polish-Lithuanian Sejm who elected him king soon after. Sânpaul was one of the few pitched battles of this period which illustrates the importance of field artillery. Bekes lost the confrontation because he assumed a defensive position without having enough firepower to hold it. Báthory had learned his lesson more than a decade ago, in the battle of Hodod (1562), and did not

---

40 Bethlen, *Historia*, vol. II, pp.296–297.
41 Szilágyi, 'Békes Gáspár', p.114.
42 Bethlen, *Historia*, vol. II, pp.309–316; Veress (ed.), *Documente*, vol. II, pp.67–69.

hesitate to act offensively, employing his light and semi-heavy cavalry with great efficiency.

These events were followed by almost two decades of relative peace and stability. Stephen Báthory was elected king of the Polish-Lithuanian Commonwealth and Transylvania was governed by his brother, Cristofer Báthory. The Habsburgs avoided undertaking any military actions against Transylvania, except some minor skirmishes in the north-western borderlands. The army was kept in good condition and regular musters were organised. Many nobles and common soldiers accompanied Báthory to Poland and fought in the siege of Gdansk (1577) and the Muscovite campaigns (1579–1582). Gaspar Bekes, his former rival, became one of his most trusted officers in the Polish-Lithuanian army. Relations with the Ottoman Empire were good, and Transylvania was regarded as a reliable vassal of the Porte.

Transylvania and the Long Turkish War (1591–1606)

Sigismund Báthory, son of Cristofer and nephew of the Polish-Lithuanian King Stephen, inherited the Transylvanian throne in 1586. Born in 1572, Sigismund was too young to rule, therefore a group of influential nobles governed the country in his name.

Border conflicts between the Habsburgs and the Ottomans grew in intensity and the two empires engaged in a prolonged conflict in 1591. It soon became clear that Transylvania would be unable to avoid this war. Most of the country was intent on continuing the pro-Ottoman policy of Stephen Báthory, but the young Prince had different plans. Although he was not yet able to rule with complete authority, Sigismund was ready to join the Holy League. Gradually, he gathered a strong faction of nobles willing to support his plans. Among them were his uncle, Stephen Bocskai, and the veterans of the Polish campaigns like Moses Székely and Albert Király.

The Christian population of the Banat area rebelled against Ottoman rule in 1594. Unable to begin direct hostilities against the Turks at the time, Sigismund Báthory supported the rebels through some of his borderland military officials, including György Palatics, the ban of Lugoj and Caransebeș, and Ferencz Geszti, captain of Deva fortress. After some minor victories against local Turkish garrisons, the Serbian insurgents were defeated by the troops of the Grand Vizier, Sinan Pasha.[43] In the meantime, Prince Sigismund was making preparation to eliminate those who opposed the anti-Ottoman war. On 28 August, with the help of his court army, he imprisoned or executed his most determined political adversaries. With full control over the Transylvanian army Sigismund was ready to declare war on his liege lord, the sultan.

By the end of 1594, Transylvania became a member of the Holy League and began negotiations with Wallachia and Moldavia. An alliance between the three Ottoman vassals was considered essential for the success of the

---

43 Feneșan, 'Din premisele', pp.100–116.

Eques Walachus.

Ein Reuter auss der Walachi 53

Sixteenth-century Wallachian horseman. Engraving by Abraham de Bruyn.

war. In this phase of the conflict Transylvanian troops were dispatched in three directions; south into Wallachia, east to Moldavia and to the south-western border in the villayet of Timişoara.

The Autumn Campaign in Wallachia, 1595

During the first half of 1595, Sigismund Báthory and his close allies, Aron Vodă of Moldavia and Michael the Brave of Wallachia, organised several incursions into Ottoman territories and were thus able to reduce pressure on the Habsburg frontier in Hungary. The Ottoman response was a campaign directed against Wallachia. Michael the Brave attacked the Turkish vanguard at Călugăreni, on 23 August, but was forced to retreat north and join forces with his Transylvanian ally.

A massive concentration of troops was organised on the southern frontier of Transylvania, near the town of Braşov. Sigismund Báthory left Alba Iulia on 27 August, at the head of a small army of 8,000 soldiers. He reached the camp of Codlea, the designated place of muster, on 3 September. Many Székely soldiers and simple peasants joined the army because the prince promised to restore their privileges. A large number, 14,700, was already in camp when the Prince arrived and 6,300 more joined them during the following days. Among the 22,000 Székelys, only 8,200 were armed with firearms while the rest carried spears and scythes. Stephen Bocskai, captain of Oradea fortress, arrived in camp with 800 cavalry and 1,200 infantry armed with arquebuses. The Moldavian ruler, Ştefan Răzvan, joined the main army on 24 September with 2,300 infantry, 700 horsemen and 22 cannons. Emperor Rudolf II had also dispatched a large detachment of 1,500 Silesian heavy cavalry clad in black armour. The Saxons mobilised companies of infantry according to their custom. The towns of Sibiu and Braşov sent 1,000 soldiers in black and blue clothes. The other smaller Saxon towns organised a combined detachment of 500 infantry. The core of this military force was the court army (guard) of the prince, consisting of 1,000 'blue guardsmen' on foot and 2,000 hussars led by the captain of the court cavalry, Gaspar Sibrik. The counties provided 2,000 cavalry and 1,000 infantry, while some of the most prominent members of the nobility were able to gather small retinues of over 100 men (Stephen Bocskai: 300, Chancellor Stephen Jósika: 200, Ladislau Gyulafi: 200, Stephen Csáky: 100). Artillery consisted of 10 large siege guns brought from Alba Iulia and 53 smaller guns (bombards, falconets and culverins). The baggage train was made up of 148 carriages with gunpowder and shot and 3,718 carriages with food and fodder. This army of reportedly 20,000 cavalry and 32,000 infantry

The siege of Târgoviște, October 1595.

was undoubtedly the largest military force yet mustered in the Principality of Transylvania.[44]

In October, after one month of preparations, Prince Sigismund and his vast army crossed the Carpathians and joined Michael the Brave. In the meantime, Sinan Pasha was able to take control over most of Wallachia and was expecting his enemies behind the walls of the fortified town of Târgoviște. When he found out about the size of the opposing army, he decided to retreat southwards and left behind a large garrison of 8,000 janissary infantry and sipahi cavalry. Sigismund could not ignore such a large force, which would threaten his rear in the event that he decided to pursue the main Turkish army, and decided to take Târgoviște first. Sources give a new detailed description of the Christian armies and their position on the battlefield. The Wallachian ruler, Michael the Brave, commanded the vanguard of 1,500 lancers and 1,000 mounted arquebusiers. They were followed by a large infantry detachment, which included most of the Saxon and Székely footmen, armed with arquebuses and short spears, organised in companies of 200 men each. The Silesian cavalry was divided into two groups and protected the flanks. Most of the artillery, consisting of 60 guns, was positioned behind the infantry line.

---

44 Crăciun, 'Scrisoarea lui Petru Pellérdi', p.498.

The siege of Giurgiu fortress, October 1595.

The second line of battle was commanded by the Moldavian ruler, Ştefan Razvan with 1,500 mounted lancers, positioned in the centre. The right flank was secured by a small detachment of Italian mercenaries sent from Tuscany under the command of Captain Silvio Piccolomini, and 150 Cossack mercenaries. Two thousand Transylvanian hussars and another group of 200 Cossacks defended the left flank. The Cossack mercenaries were described as being very similar to Tatars, armed with sabres, bows, long arquebuses, mounted on small horses with high saddles and short stirrups.

The Transylvanian Prince assumed command of the reaguard, organised in three squadrons. The first consisted of 4,000 cavalry bearing red flags with the heraldry of the Holy Roman Empire and the three dragon teeth of the Báthory family. The other two squadrons of 500 cavalry each acted as the personal guard of the prince. The baggage train was last, and was defended by six infantry companies.[45]

The besiegers organised a fortified camp in the vicinity of Târgovişte. On the following day, Sigismund Báthory ordered a general assault on the fortifications. The wooden ramparts were set on fire and the Christian

---

45 Andrei Veress, 'Campania creştinilor în contra lui Sinan Paşa din 1595', *Academia Română. Memoriile secţiunii istorice*, IV: 3 (1925), pp.87, 103–104; Radu R. Rosetti, *Istoria artei militare a românilor până la mijlocul veacului al XVII-lea* (Bucureşti: Corint, 2003), pp.403–408.

soldiers were able to scale the walls with ladders. The Ottoman garrison surrendered soon after. Two large cannons and 44 falconets were captured on this occasion. Filippo Pigafetta, one of the Italian mercenaries in the Transylvanian army, recorded these events, and also added interesting observations regarding the weapons and fighting style of local soldiers. According to his reports, gunpowder weapons were rather rare while most soldiers carried half-pikes, scythes and other close combat weapons.[46]

The Transylvanian army, together with their Wallachian and Moldavian allies, continued to march towards the Danube, in pursuit of Sinan Pasha. The last significant moment of this campaign was the siege of Giurgiu fortress on the Danube. Ottoman soldiers, burdened by captives and other spoils of war, were eager to return home. Most of the army was preparing to cross the river when the Transylvanian vanguard reached the fortress. Giurgiu was besieged for three days while the artillery and the infantry of Sigismund Báthory inflicted many casualties on those who were still attempting to cross the river. In the last day of the siege the wooden ramparts of the fortress were set on fire, and soon after Transylvanian soldiers stormed the fortress and were able to take it without suffering too many casualties.[47]

The large army of Sigismund Báthory, and his Wallachian and Moldavian allies, obtained a strategic victory against an Ottoman army unwilling to engage in open combat. Direct confrontations between the two enemies were rather brief with few casualties. The Christians lost more soldiers to hunger and cold than in combat. Báthory had achieved his objective, the Ottomans retreated south of the Danube, but Wallachia was seriously affected by raids and destructions. On 29 November, the Prince of Transylvania made his triumphal entrance into Alba Iulia convinced that he had won a great victory. The representatives of the estates feared the retaliation of the Porte. Some of the most important Turkish captives were set free to deliver a peace proposition to the sultan.

The Siege of Timişoara, 1596

The year 1596 began with a rebellion of the Székely. Sigismund Báthory was unable, or maybe unwilling, to keep the promise to restore the privileges of this community. The uprising was defeated by Stephen Bocskai while the Prince travelled to Prague, to meet with Emperor Rudolph II. With a small but efficient army of court guards and nobles, Bocskai lead a swift and cruel repression, known as the 'The Bloody Carnival'.[48] Peace negotiations with the Turks were abandoned and the Transylvanian army was making preparations for another year of hostilities. Some detachments were sent south in Wallachia, to aid Michael the Brave, while most of the troops were directed towards the border with the Ottoman province of Timişoara.

Borderland raids and skirmishes were common occurrences during times of peace. Since the official start of the war, such small-scale military actions were more frequent and involved larger groups of combatants.

---

46   Ardelean, *Organizarea militară*, p.276.
47   Veress, 'Campania creştinilor', pp.90–91; Bethlen, *Historia*, vol. III, pp.623–628.
48   *Memorialul lui Nagy Szabó Ferencz*, pp.78–80.

Some of these raids gained notoriety and were briefly described in German and Italian *avvisi* (newspapers of that period). An attack of Transylvanian border troops on a convoy of the Pasha from Timișoara was considered a resounding success. The soldiers of Sigismund Báthory killed 300 Turkish soldiers in the skirmish and liberated 160 women taken into slavery by the Turks. Three hundred horses and 13 wagons with various precious goods were also captured on this occasion.[49]

The siege of Timișoara was carefully prepared during the previous year (1595), when 11 fortifications from the Banat area were captured by Transylvanian troops, including the important fortress of Lipova. Once again, Prince Sigismund Báthory decided to personally lead his army, estimated to be about 40,000 men strong.[50] The troops, gathered in the vicinity of Alba Iulia, began their march along the Mureş valley on 21 May. Six days later they reached Lipova where a small Turkish force, attempting to take the fortress, was defeated. After a few days of rest the Transylvanian army continued to advance towards their main objective, Timișoara. As soon as the vanguard approached the fortifications of the town, on 10 June, they were attacked by the Turkish garrison. The troops of Prince Sigismund were victorious, and the siege began. During the next day a Diet was summoned by Báthory to discuss organisational aspects and to request more financial and military support from the Estates.[51]

The Transylvanians tried to organise a blockade of the fortress, but this was very difficult because of the marshy terrain that surrounded Timișoara. Trenches were dug and three main artillery platforms were built. Twenty siege cannons bombarded the walls of Timișoara for six days, until 16 June, when a breach in the wall was made. Báthory could not take advantage of this achievement because a significant number of Tatars and Turks attacked his army from outside the fortifications. The general assault on the fortress was postponed as most of the Transylvanian cavalry had to deal with this secondary threat. The Prince himself led the cavalry charge and was successful in diving his enemies away. A general assault on the fortress was then attempted on 23 June, but the Turkish garrison was able to build a wooden rampart behind the collapsed section of the wall and successfully repelled the attack. In the meantime, news that a larger Ottoman army was heading towards Timișoara reached the camp of the Transylvanian army and on 24 June Prince Sigismund decided to retreat.[52]

The failed siege of Timișoara was the first major setback for Sigismund Báthory, one that would undermine his confidence in the ability of the Holy

---

49 Veress (ed.), *Documente*, vol. V, pp.13–17.
50 Bernardino Beccari da Sacile alla Minerva, *La rotta che ha datta il Serenissimo Prencipe di Transilvania &c. a'i Turchi e Tartari sotto Temesuar alli 17. Di Giugno 1596* (Roma: appresso Nicolo Mutii, MDXCVI), pp.1–5.
51 *MCRT*, vol. III, pp.501–504.
52 Bernardino Beccari da Sacile alla Minerva, *Ragguaglio di tutto l'assedio di Temesvar Fino all levata del Serenissimo Prencipe di Transilvania da quella piazza, Dove s'intendono tre notabili fattioni di Sua Altezza contra i Turchi, et Tartari, Et in particolare la morte del Tartaro Cane pe mano dell'Altezza Sua, & l'acquisto delle sue bagaglie, & della preda che haveva fatta. Seguita a di 19.Giugno 1596* (Roma: Per Nicoló Mutii, 1596), pp.1–6.

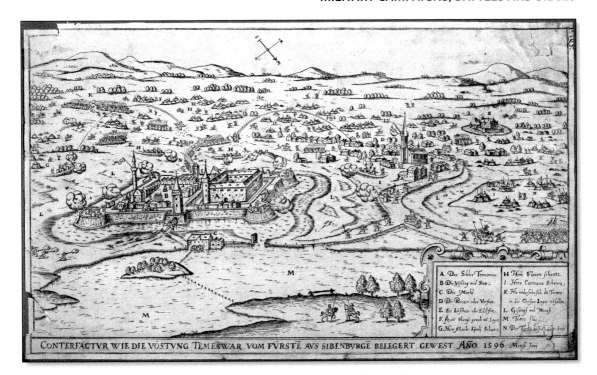

CONTERFACTVR WIE DIE VÖSTVNG TEMESWAR VOM FVRSTE AVS SIBENBVRGE BELEGERT GEWEST AÑO. 1596. Menß Junÿ

A. Das Schloß Temeswar.
B. Die Vöstung vnd Statt.
C. Die Mühl.
D. Die Reußen oder Vorstatt.
E. Ein Lustheuß oder Eddlsitz.
F. so vil Hungÿ gezelt vñ Leger.
G. Herr Allbrecht Kornis Schantz.
H. Herrn Flosen schantz.
I. Herrn Carmozan Schantz.
K. Hie vnderstehn sich die Tartern in der Christen Leger zufallen.
L. Gstümpf vnd Morast.
M. Temes fluß.
N. Der Türken vssfall wider die Statt.

League to win the war with the Ottomans. Although the Prince of Transylvania mobilised a vast military force, he was unable to take a well-defended and well-provisioned Ottoman fortification. The defensive potential of Timişoara was enhanced by the surrounding marshland that made effective encirclement very difficult. The campaign and the siege followed an established pattern that included the capture of minor fortifications in the vicinity of the main objective, an attempt to organise a blockade of the fortification, and sustained artillery fire that produced a breach in the wall followed by a general assault. An important factor that eventually led to the Ottoman victory was the presence of a mobile cavalry force (mostly Tatars) outside the fortress, which exerted constant pressure on the besiegers and diverted their attention. The Transylvanian artillery had proven its efficiency and managed to create a breach in the wall. Nevertheless a large part of the Transylvanian army consisted of light and semi-heavy (hussars) cavalry which were at a disadvantage in the marshy terrain that surrounded Timişoara. After 14 days of siege, Báthory retreated in order to avoid a confrontation with a larger Ottoman force that was heading his way. However, Sultan Mehmet III had other intentions. His objective was the fortress of Eger in Upper Hungary. The Habsburgs were able to attack the Ottoman army only after the fortress was lost on the battlefield of Mezőkeresztes. Prince Sigismund joined the Habsburg army and his Transylvanian troops fought in the vanguard. The battle lasted two days (25–26 October) and ended with a disastrous defeat of the Christian armies.[53]

The army of the Transylvanian Prince besieging Timişoara in 1596, engraving by Hans Johan Siebmacher. (National Museum of Banat, Timişoara, România)

---

53 Komáromy, *A Mezőkeresztesi csata*, pp.281–284.

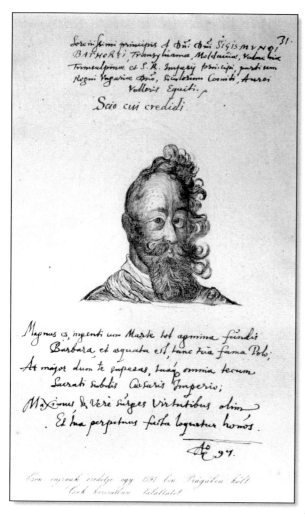

A portrait of Sigismund Báthory followed by a short poem dedicated to him, Prague, 1597. (The National Museum of Transylvanian History, Cluj-Napoca, Romania)

Sigismund Báthory returned to Transylvania but his determination to fight against the Turks was considerably weakened. Another attempt to take Timişoara was made the following year, in 1597. Chancellor Stephen Josika was entrusted with the leadership of the besieging force, but he was unable to take the town.

The Battle of Şelimbăr, 28 October 1599

The war was not going well for Transylvania and her allies. Sigismund Báthory decided to abandon the country and the responsibility of leadership in December 1597. The Habsburgs appointed three commissioners to govern the country and tried to rally the estates to their cause. Many were reluctant to fight for the Habsburgs and were willing to reassume their role as faithful Ottoman vassals. In 1598 a Turkish army besieged the fortress of Oradea but was forced to withdraw because of bad weather. Prince Sigismund returned to Transylvania in August 1598, only to abdicate again several months later, in March 1599. He left the throne to his cousin, Cardinal Andrew Báthory, who enjoyed Polish support and was willing to abandon the Holy League. In this context, driven by the necessity to maintain Transylvania in the anti-Ottoman league, Michael the Brave of Wallachia crossed the Carpathians and engaged the army of Andrew Báthory on the battlefield of Şelimbăr, near the Saxon town of Sibiu.

The ruler of Wallachia was an accomplished military commander, leading an experienced army of locals and foreign mercenaries. In spite of their various origins, they had spent a few years campaigning together and had a sense of cohesion that could only be acquired on the battlefield. Michael the Brave gathered his troops near the town Ploieşti, close to the Transylvanian border. Their total number has been estimated at about 20,000 combatants, a number that also included large groups of Székely and other Transylvanians who joined the army of the Wallachian ruler after he crossed the mountains. The backbone of his army consisted of local boyars and their retinues, and a semi-privileged group of horsemen known as 'curteni' the equivalent of the Transylvanian court cavalry (*praetorianum aequitatum quos illi Kurtanos vocant*). Serbian (*rascianos*), Polish and Cossack mercenaries are also mentioned by contemporary sources. A large detachment of 5,000 infantry included local soldiers and foreign troops among whom a significant proportion were *hajdús* from the Transylvanian and Hungarian frontier. More than 1,000 Hungarian and Transylvanian nobles were already in his camp before he departed from Ploieşti, and others joined him before the

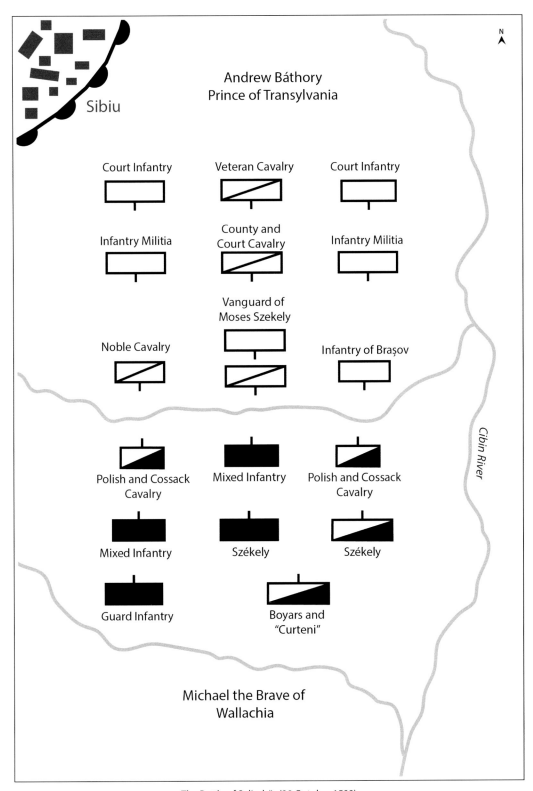

The Battle of Şelimbăr (28 October 1599).

battle began.[54] Michael the Brave organised his troops in three battle lines. A large infantry detachment was positioned in the centre of the first line, flanked by 4,000 Polish and Cossack cavalry. The second line consisted of one infantry detachment armed with spears and other close combat weapons, a mixed detachment of 2,500 Moldavian soldiers and the Székely cavalry and infantry. The Wallachian voivode personally commanded the last battle line consisting of 3,000 chosen infantry and 2,000 cavalry.[55]

His opponent, Cardinal Andrew Báthory, had chosen a similar approach and also organised his troops in three lines. His army was significantly smaller (about 9,000 men) because many Transylvanians had joined the Wallachian army. Even some of his foreign mercenaries chose to defect to the enemy, a group of 600 Cossacks making this decision on the eve of battle. The vanguard of the Transylvanian army consisted of 1,000 Székely cavalry led by Moses Székely, followed by 1,600 infantry armed with arquebuses. The right flank was secured by a cavalry detachment while the left flank was held by the infantry of Brașov. Most of the Transylvanian cavalry (about 3,000 men), the county nobility and the court cavalry, was positioned in the centre of the second battle line. Two infantry detachments, 1,000 men each, defended the flanks. Behind them a chosen group of 600 veteran cavalry (*triarii*) and two more detachments of infantry, 1,000 men each, protected the Transylvanian Prince.[56]

The battle began with an exchange of artillery fire. The Transylvanian vanguard advanced towards the enemy and the cavalry charged the centre of the first enemy line, which consisted of a large body of infantry. The swift cavalry action was successful, and the infantry of the Wallachian ruler was about to disperse when the Polish and Cossack cavalry from the flanks came to their aid. The remaining Transylvanian cavalry was forced to retreat. In the second phase of the battle, Michael the Brave rallied his Wallachian, Serbian, Polish and Hungarian cavalry and lead a devastating charge on the second Transylvanian battle line. Taking advantage of his superior numbers and momentum, voivode Michael was able to overwhelm the enemy cavalry. Gaspar Kornis, the captain general, and other leading members of the Transylvanian nobility were captured and disarmed. Cardinal Andrew Báthory fled the battlefield but was later captured by some Székely soldiers and decapitated. The rest of Transylvanian army was routed and by sundown Michael the Brave had won a decisive victory and with it the leadership of the Transylvanian Principality.[57]

In this battle, as on previous occasions, Transylvanians were divided and fought in both armies. The political situation was rather confused, and some were willing to continue the war against the Ottomans while others believed that being vassals of the Turkish sultan was a better option. Both armies had a similar composition with a slightly larger proportion of cavalry. The

54 Bethlen, Historia, vol. IV, pp.334–335; Nicolae Iorga, *Documente nouă, în mare parte românești, relative la Petru Șchiopul și Mihai Viteazul* (București: Institutul de Arte Grafice Carol Göbl, 1898), pp.34–36.
55 Veress (ed.), *Documente*, vol. V, pp.338–340.
56 Crăciun, *Cronicarul Szamosközy*, pp.123–126.
57 Bethlen, *Historia*, vol. IV, pp.400–406.

battle was decided by numerical superiority, through the impact of a fierce frontal cavalry assault. The infantry, although mostly armed with firearms, played only a supporting role. It was one of the few battles fought in this war with significant political consequences. Under the leadership of Michael the Brave, Transylvania remained a member of the Holy League and the Habsburgs enjoyed the benefits of maintaining a secondary front against the Ottomans,[58] one that would reduce the pressure on the Hungarian border.

The Battle of Mirăslău, 18–19 September 1600

In 1600, Michael the Brave maintained his rule over Transylvania and was also able to occupy Moldavia after a swift military campaign. For a short while he ruled over the three small buffer states that divided the Habsburgs, the Ottomans and the Polish-Lithuanian Commonwealth. His success was short lived because a strong faction of Transylvanian nobles, led by Stephen Csáki of Cheresig, was preparing to overthrow him. Giorgio Basta, a Habsburg general of Albanian origin, was also approaching the Transylvanian border from the north-west.

Michael gathered his troops in a camp near the Saxon town of Sebeş, while Csáki and his supporters gathered in Turda. Transylvania was once again divided, and soldiers began to move from one camp to another. A group of 700 Cossack mercenaries deserted the army of the Wallachian voivode and joined the Transylvanian rebels after receiving wages in advance from their previous employer.[59] Csáki sent envoys to General Basta and managed to convince him that Michael was no longer a suitable ruler for Transylvania or a reliable ally of the Habsburgs. On 14 September, 6,000 Habsburg mercenaries joined the Transylvanian rebels. They were German and Hungarian infantry from the borders armed with muskets and heavy cavalry from Silesia armed with pistols and swords. The Transylvanian rebels were mostly cavalry from the counties and detachments of infantry provided by some of the towns. Bistriţa, for example, sent 700 infantry and provisions.[60] Together they managed to organise a strong army of 12,000 infantry and 6,000 cavalry.

Michael was unable to gather all his troops together on the battlefield. Some of his captains, like Baba Novac and Deli Marko, were unable to reach him in time.[61] The alliance between Csáky and Basta had taken him by surprise, and he was forced to muster his available troops on a hillside overlooking the Mureş river, in the vicinity of a village called Mirăslău. His

58 Ovidiu Cristea, 'A Second Front: Wallachia and the "Long War" against the Turks', Gábor Kárman, Radu G. Păun (eds) *Europe and the Ottoman World. Exchanges and Conflicts (sixteenth and seventeenth centuries)* (Istanbul: The Isis Press, 2013), pp.13–27.

59 Veress (ed.), *Documente*, vol. VI, p.165.

60 Liviu Cîmpeanu, 'Liga nobiliară de la Turda şi revoluţia', Transilvaniei împotriva lui Mihai Vodă (1–18 septembrie 1600), *Anuarul Institutului de Cercetări Socio-Umane Sibiu*, vol. XXIV (2017), p 47.

61 Liviu Cîmpeanu, 'Consecinţele războiului asupra populaţiei civile: cazul luptelor din Transilvania în toamna anului 1600, după căderea lui Mihai Viteazul', *Anuarul Institutului de Cercetări Socio-Umane Sibiu*, vol. XXIII (2016), pp.28–29.

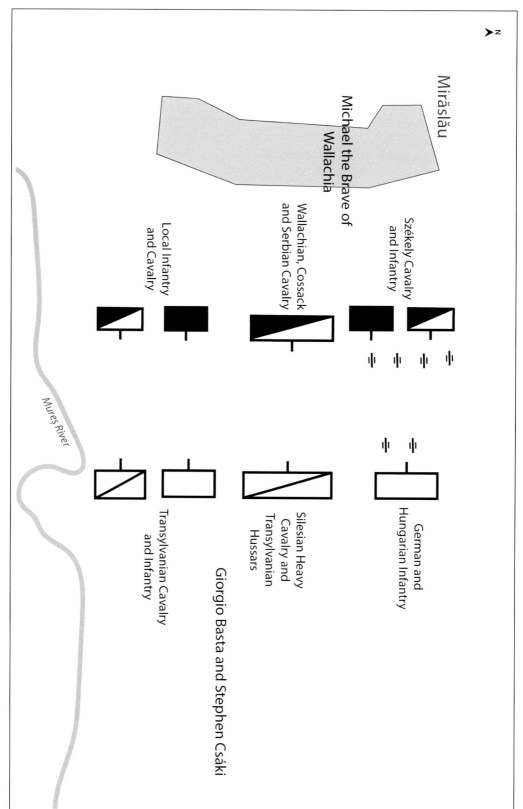

The Battle of Mirăslău (18–19 September 1600).

army consisted of Székely, Cossacks, Serbians and hastily recruited local infantry, about 12,000 men in total.[62]

Basta and his Transylvanian allies were advancing towards Alba Iulia when they meet some scouting parties sent by the Wallachian voivode. The Transylvanian hussars defeated a large group of Cossack cavalry in the vicinity of the enemy camp. Encouraged by their victory they wanted to assault the camp of Michael the Brave the same evening, but Basta convinced them to wait until the next day.[63] An artillery duel began in the morning and things were going in favour of the Wallachian ruler, because he held the high ground. Understanding his tactical disadvantage, Basta decided to lure the enemy away from his favourable position. His plan was to fake a retreat in the hopes that Michael would follow. The Transylvanian nobles were against such a shameful proposition, arguing that their soldiers would lose morale while their enemy would gain confidence. The Habsburg officers insisted that such subtleties were common in modern strategy while pointing out that both Transylvanians and Wallachians had a rudimentary understanding of warfare and were relying too much on the strength of their cavalry charges. In the end Basta won the argument and his troops performed a feigned retreat. Michael took the bait and followed his adversaries hoping to win the day with a decisive cavalry charge. That is why he had positioned most of his horsemen in the centre of the battle line, while the flanks were protected by mixed detachments of cavalry, infantry and artillery. After marching a significant distance, Basta ordered an infantry attack on the left flank of the enemy, where most of their artillery was located. The German and Hungarian musketeers defeated the Székely troops that were protecting this flank and captured most of their field guns. The main action took place in the centre, where both generals had concentrated their cavalry. The decisive blow was struck by a contingent of 1,500 Silesian heavy cavalry who discharged their pistols when they were 50 paces away from their enemies and then charged with their swords. Under such pressure, the Wallachian battle line lost cohesion and troops began to flee the battlefield. Michael the Brave himself barely escaped the battlefield and swam across the Mureș River carrying his personal banner.[64]

This defeat ended the short rule of Michael the Brave over Transylvania. Internal strife had weakened the position of the Holy League in this area and the balance between the two camps was once again restored. The battle of Mirăslău had shown the limits of the Transylvanian and Wallachian strategic approach to pitched battles. As most previous battles had shown, the Transylvanian army relied too much on its hussar cavalry. General Basta was aware of this and was able to use it to his own advantage. Victory was gained through a well-planned simulated retreat, a flanking attack performed by his infantry and the counter-attack of his heavy cavalry.

---

62 Panaitescu, *Mihai Viteazul*, p.224.
63 Bagi, 'Giorgio Basta', p.49.
64 Panaitescu, *Mihai Viteazul*, p.225; Veress (ed.), *Documente*, vol. VI, pp.205–213.

The Battle of Guruslău, 3 August 1601

The fragile alliance between the Habsburgs, represented by Giorgio Basta, and the Transylvanian estates dissolved soon after their victory over Michael the Brave. The nobility, under the leadership of the same Stephen Csáky, decided to officially declare their allegiance to the Ottoman Empire and to bring back Sigismund Báthory. At the end of March 1601, Sigismund was elected as Transylvanian Prince for the third time. Rudolf II decided to maintain control over Transylvania as well and sent reinforcements to Basta. Michael the Brave travelled to Prague and convinced the Emperor of his good will towards the Habsburgs and his intention to continue the war against the Turks. The Habsburg monarch offered him financial aid and the approval to recruit soldiers along the Habsburg borders in Hungary.

The Ottoman sultan sent 6,000 Tatars and 5,000 soldiers from Moldavia and Wallachia to aid his Transylvanian vassal. With this small army Sigismund was able to retake some fortifications on the western borders which had been occupied by Habsburg garrisons. The Transylvanian estates showed willingness to support their pro-Ottoman prince and mobilised their troops. By the beginning of August 1601, Prince Báthory gathered a large force which included local troops but also a contingent of Tatars, Moldavians and Wallachians, about 30,000 men in total.[65]

Former enemies Giorgio Basta and Michael the Brave were now forced by circumstances to fight as allies. Their armies were united in the vicinity of Satu Mare and included a large variety of locals and foreign mercenaries. Michael the Brave came with several thousand *hajdús* from the Hungarian border and smaller contingents of Serbian and Cossack mercenaries, roughly 15,000 men. Basta commanded an army of 8,000 infantry armed with firearms and 2,000 Hungarian lancers (hussars). His most trusted soldiers were the 1,500 Silesian and Walloon heavy cavalry. Together they had an army of about 26,500 men, which was slightly smaller than that of the enemy.[66]

Sigismund Báthory advanced with his army towards the fortress of Șimleu, on the north-western border of Transylvania. Although he already had a large army, he was expecting more reinforcements from the Ottomans. Basta decided to attack Sigismund before his numerical advantage would increase even more. He took personal command over the vanguard consisting of Silesian and Walloon heavy cavalry, two companies of Hungarian lancers, one company of mounted arquebusiers, the infantry regiment of Bartholomew Pezzen, three companies of Walloon infantry and six field guns. The main body included the mercenaries of Michael the Brave and five companies of mounted arquebusiers. The rearguard was commanded by Colonel Rothal with 1,000 light cavalry provided by the Wallachian voivode, three companies of mounted arquebusiers from Upper Hungary and 1,500 Hungarian infantry.

---

65 Veress, *Documente*, vol. VI, pp.420–421; Leonardus Basilius, 'Naratio De Rebus Transylvanicis (1599–1604)', Radu Constantinescu *Lupta pentru unitate națională a Țărilor Române 1590–1630. Documente externe* (București: Direcția Generală a Arhivelor Statului, Institutul de Istorie 'Nicolae Iorga', 1981), p.320.

66 Crăciun, *Cronicarul Szamosközy*, p.151; Veress (ed.), *Documente*, vol. VI, p.423.

Unfortunately sources are not that generous in details when describing the Transylvanian army. When he found out that the Habsburgs were advancing towards the border, Prince Sigismund moved further north in search of an advantageous battlefield. He eventually chose a forested area with some high hills and deep gorges near the village of Guruslău. The two armies met on 3 August around 9:00 a.m. The Transylvanians held the higher ground and had 42 field artillery pieces. The exchange of gunfire was going in their favour, but they hesitated to attack the Habsburg vanguard. Two hours after noon the rest of the Habsburg army arrived on the battlefield. Because his soldiers were exhausted after a long march, Basta and the other commanders decided to wait until the next day. At 5:00 p.m. the Transylvanian army began to retreat without any obvious reason. The Habsburg army was ready for battle with Basta on the left flank, Michael the Brave on the right flank and Colonel Rothal with his troops in the centre. When he saw the enemy retreating, Basta decided to attack. He advanced with 600 musketeers on his left flank against the enemy artillery. They occupied a favourable position on the edge of a deep gorge to avoid a frontal assault from the Transylvanian cavalry. In the meantime both Rothal and Michael the Brave attacked the Transylvanian infantry defending the hill where their artillery was positioned. Overwhelmed by the Habsburg cavalry charge, the infantry ran from the battlefield and left the guns unprotected. When the Transylvanian cavalry returned on the battlefield, they were met by salvos of musket fire on their right flank. With the artillery already captured by the enemy, Sigismund decided to retreat. Most of his horsemen were able to escape the battlefield but many of his foot soldiers were killed or captured by the Habsburgs.[67]

Sigismund Báthory lost this battle because he was hesitant. Although he had numerical superiority, he was uncertain of the value of his soldiers and was expecting more reinforcements from the Ottomans. He lost an excellent opportunity when he decided not to attack the Habsburg vanguard. The battlefield, dominated by hills and gorges, was not well suited for cavalry combat. The Habsburg infantry performed very well in this environment by taking advantage of natural obstacles. Although the pro-Ottoman faction was defeated on the battlefield the Habsburgs were not able to take full control of the country. Tensions between Basta and Michael the Brave increased and soon after the battle, the Wallachian voivode was assassinated by Walloon soldiers. Sigismund Báthory reorganised his forces and initiated a war of attrition against his Habsburg enemies.

The Battle of Brașov, 17 July 1603

As winter was setting in at end of 1601 Transylvania remained a divided country. The northern half was controlled by General Basta, while the southern regions acknowledged the rule of Sigismund Báthory and his pro-Ottoman policy.

---

67 Veress (ed.), *Documente*, vol. VIp.433; Ion Ardeleanu et al. (eds), *Mihai Viteazul în conștiința europeană: Documente externe* (București: Editura Academiei Republicii Socialiste România, 1982), pp.657–661.

Hostilities began once more in the spring of 1602. After a few short sieges and skirmishes, Basta was able to extend his control further south, while Prince Sigismund was cornered in the fortress of Deva, on the south-western frontier. With his authority diminishing by the day, Sigismund Báthory gave up, for the last time, on the title of Prince of Transylvania. The leadership of the pro-Ottoman faction in Transylvania was assumed by Moses Székely, who took refuge in Turkish territory. At the end of 1602, Basta controlled most of Transylvania with an army of 6,000 Habsburg mercenaries, 3,000 Székely soldiers and 1,000 mounted nobles.[68]

The winter of 1602–1603 was very harsh and the resources of the country were exhausted after consecutive years of war. Under these circumstances Basta was forced to send almost half of his troops to Hungary.[69] Taking advantage of this situation, Moses Székely returned to Transylvania and rallied all those who were willing to overthrow the Habsburg rule. The Banat of Lugoj and Caransebeş and the County of Hunedoara accepted his authority without opposition. Giorgio Basta decided to avoid a direct confrontation and retreated north. One by one the towns, seats, districts and counties of Transylvania accepted the new rule. Székely was accompanied by a large army of Tatars. After gathering enough spoils and over 10,000 captives, most of them departed home, leaving the country in a miserable state.[70]

Moses Székely was elected prince with the consent of the Ottomans, but his authority over Transylvania was challenged by the ruler of Wallachia, Radu Şerban, a trusted ally of the Habsburgs. His troops crossed the Carpathians and attacked the army of the new Transylvanian prince. Some of the Székelys decided to join the troops of Radu Şerban even though Moses was one of their own. The final confrontation took place on 17 July 1603, near the town of Braşov, after four days of skirmishing.

Prince Moses organised a fortified camp on the Bârsa River, near a paper mill that supplied the town of Braşov. He commanded a small army of 11,250 soldiers, composed of 4,000 Tatars, 1,000 Turks under Becteş Pasha, a mixed detachment of 6,000 cavalry and infantry provided by the Székely and the nobility of the counties, 200 infantry from the town of Braşov and 25 field guns. Some of his troops and the artillery were positioned inside a camp surrounded by wagons. The Transylvanian Prince deployed about 700 wagons in a rectangle, to defend his artillery from a cavalry charge. The so-called 'wagenburg' (wagon fortress) tactic was established during the Hussite Wars in the first half of the fifteenth century and was later adopted by the army of the Hungarian kingdom and other neighbouring states, including the Ottoman Empire.[71] All those involved in this battle were familiar with this tactical approach, with its advantages and weaknesses. The Tatar and

---

68 Veress (ed.), *Documente*, vol. VII, pp.75–76.
69 Veress (ed.), *Documente*, VII, pp.119–120.
70 Basilius, 'Naratio', pp.345–346.
71 Gábor Ágoston, 'Behind the Turkish war machine: gunpowder technology and war industry in the Ottoman Empire, 1450–1700', Brett D. Steele, Tamera Dorland, *The Heirs of Archimedes: Science and the Art of War through the Age of Enlightenment* (Cambridge Massachusetts: MIT Press, 2005), p.112.

Turkish cavalry, together with 300 Transylvanian riders, waited outside, on the right flank of the fortified camp.

Radu Șerban had a larger army of about 14,000 soldiers. His troops were organised in two lines. The vanguard had an infantry detachment in the centre and cavalry on the flanks. The Wallachian voivode waited in the rearguard with his best troops. He took the initiative and attacked the enemy cavalry deployed outside the fortified camp with the troops on his left flank. The Turks and the Tatars were not well enough motivated to risk their lives in an open battle and decided to flee, although they held a numerical advantage.

The fortified camp of Moses Székely was situated on marshy terrain. Considering this specific condition Radu Șerban ordered his cavalry to dismount and they assaulted the fortified camp on foot. The attackers took advantage of natural obstacles such as trees and overgrown bushes and were able to approach the enemy camp without too many losses. The Wallachian infantry overcame the defensive obstacles and slaughtered most of the troops inside. The Prince lost his life in the melee, thus becoming the first, but not the last, Transylvanian ruler who died on the battlefield.[72]

This battle marked yet another political change for Transylvania, leading to the restoration of Habsburg authority. Moses Székely was an experienced military commander, of humble origin, who made his way to the top of the hierarchy through political skill and military prowess. He lost the battle with Radu Șerban because he miscalculated the effectiveness of a fortified camp in those particular conditions. Instead of offering protection, the 'wagenburg' hindered his mobility and the cohesion of his heterogeneous army. The outcome of the battle was decided at the moment the Tatars and the Turkish cavalry left the battlefield. Without cavalry support from the outside, the fortified camp was overwhelmed by an army of light infantry which also had the advantage of numbers on their side.

The last years of the Long Turkish War were dominated by the rebellion of Stephen Bocskai (1604–1606). The *hajdús* from the border areas made up the bulk of his army. Most conflict with Habsburg troops took place in Royal Hungary, beyond the frontiers of Transylvania.

The Long Turkish War was a difficult test of endurance for the young Transylvanian state and for its military organisation. The performance of the Transylvanian army in this conflict was affected by two main factors; poor leadership and political division. Sigismund Báthory entered the war with great enthusiasm but he was unable to deal with his first failures on the battlefield. He willingly gave up on the throne and then changed his mind three times in four years. The other elected rulers, Andrew Báthory, Michael the Brave and Moses Székely, had very short reigns and were unable to consolidate their authority. The country was constantly divided between the two political options represented by the Habsburgs and the Ottomans. In this war, the Transylvanian army was rarely fully mobilised in the same camp. On most occasions Transylvanians fought against each other, according to the ever-shifting allegiance of the estates they represented.

---

72 Rosetti, *Istoria artei militare*, pp.349–353; Ardelean, *Organizarea militară*, pp.297–298.

A clear improvement was made in the field of siege warfare. During the 1595 autumn campaign in Wallachia, Prince Sigismund and his allies were able to capture the main fortifications which stood in their way, Târgovişte and Giurgiu. The two sieges of Timişoara (1596 and 1597) were failures, but during the first siege, the Transylvanian artillery was able to breach the defensive wall of the Ottoman fortification.

Most of the major pitched battles, like Şelimbăr (1599), Guruslău (1601) and Braşov (1603) were lost. The Transylvanians, like all their neighbours in central and south-eastern Europe, relied too much on their cavalry which, in spite of its great mobility, was usually deployed in the centre of the battle line and charged the enemy head-on. Field artillery, although present in most battles, was ineffective. The infantry was well supplied with firearms but lacked defensive pike formations and was thus vulnerable to enemy cavalry charges.

In spite of these obvious shortcomings, Transylvania and its neighbours, Wallachia and Moldavia, played a very important role in this large-scale confrontation between empires. When they joined the war in 1595 on the side of the Habsburgs, they considerably reduced the Ottoman pressure on the Hungarian border. The lower Danube area became a secondary theatre of war, where the Ottomans were forced to assume a defensive stance, at least during the early years. The various forms of irregular warfare, like raids and skirmishes, typical for such border areas had an important role in the balance of war. The incursions performed by Michael the Brave south of the Danube and the Transylvanian raids on the neighbouring Ottoman province of Timişoara were considered great achievements in the conflict with the 'Turkish infidels'.

The Military Campaigns of Prince Gabriel Báthory (1608–1613)

The young and ambitious Gabriel Báthory was elected prince in 1608, after the short reign of Sigismund Rákóczi. He was supported by the borderland *hajdús*, who had gained a semi-privileged position during the reign of Stephen Bocskai. From the beginning, Báthory wanted to build a strong and loyal army, which would help him achieve his political objectives.

The new Prince of Transylvania wanted to rule like an absolute monarch and many of his contemporaries considered him a tyrant. By 1610 he had a large military force of about 20,000 soldiers. Most of them were *hajdús* who owed their allegiance to the Prince and were beyond the control of the Estates. During the same year, Báthory and his soldiers occupied the town of Sibiu. Their first concern was to take control of the well supplied arsenal in the town.[73] The Transylvanian Saxons were outraged by this abusive behaviour, and tried to overthrow the Prince through all means available.

Báthory also planned to take control of the neighbouring Romanian principalities. His first step was to attack Wallachia in the winter of 1610/1611.

---

73 Kraus, *Cronica*, pp.7–9.

While his armies were gathering in the vicinity of Sibiu, envoys were sent to the Ottoman sultan asking for approval and support in this political venture. On this occasion, the bulk of the Transylvanian army consisted of *hajdús* from the western border. The nobles of Lugoj and Caransebeş answered the Prince's summons in great numbers. The Székely Seats also sent detachments in the hopes that this belligerent ruler would restore their privileges. Depending upon which sources are to be believed the total size of the army varied between 7,000 and 35,000. Throughout the first two weeks of December, soldiers gathered at the southern border of Transylvania although it was a very cold winter. Crossing the Carpathians was a slow and hazardous endeavour because of the heavy snowfall.[74] Radu Şerban, the ruler of Wallachia, decided to avoid a direct confrontation at the time and retreated towards the Moldavian border in the east. The Transylvanian army captured Târgovişte without encountering too much opposition. While most of the army remained encamped there, smaller detachments were sent to subdue the other regions of the country. The locals were willing to accept the new leadership while some of the Serbian mercenaries and Wallachian boyars joined the army of the Transylvanian Prince. Things were going well for Báthory until the envoys sent to the Istanbul returned with unsettling news. The Sultan considered that his vassals beyond the Danube should be satisfied with the rule of their own countries and decided to support a new pretender on the throne of Wallachia, Radu Mihnea.[75]

Gabriel Báthory remained in Wallachia until the end of March 1611, when his army began to disintegrate. Turkish troops attacked the territories of the *hajdús* in the borderlands and as a result the soldiers of the Transylvanian Prince decided to return home to defend their lands and families.[76] Many *hajdús* lived beyond the Transylvanian border in Hungary and were thus subjects of the Habsburgs. Their solidarity with the Transylvanian Prince was perceived as an act of rebellion and the Hungarians decided to retaliate. An army, commanded by Sigismund Forgács, was sent into Transylvania under the pretext of quelling the *hajdú* rebellion.[77]

The Battle of Braşov, 10 July 1611

In the summer of 1611, Gabriel Báthory was surrounded by enemies. The Saxons and some of the nobility were ready to rebel against their prince, while Hungary, Moldavia and Wallachia were planning to attack Transylvania.

Radu Şerban of Wallachia took the first initiative and prepared to cross the mountains into Transylvania. Báthory had already sent orders of mobilisation in April and his troops began to gather, once more, on the southern border. More *hajdú* mercenaries left his army, fearing the retribution of Habsburg authorities. Nevertheless, the Transylvanian Prince was able to gather an army of significant size and guarded the most commonly used mountain passes that connected Wallachia to Transylvania. Radu Şerban chose a

---

74   Veress (ed.), *Documente*, vol. VIII, pp.111–113.
75   Veress (ed.), *Documente*, vol. VIII, pp.119–134.
76   Veress (ed.), *Documente*, vol. VIII, p.149.
77   Veress (ed.), *Documente*, vol. VIII, pp.173–181.

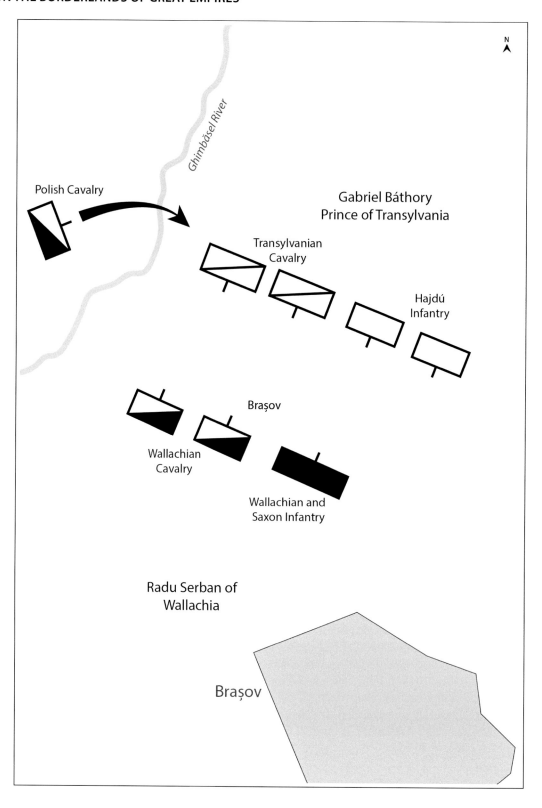

The Battle of Brașov (10 July 1611)

difficult and uncommon route across the Carpathians and approached the town of Braşov, surprising his enemy. The citizens of Braşov were eager to help the Wallachian voivode, sending provisions and troops to join his army.[78]

The two armies were of roughly equal size (about 10,000 men each), and met outside the defensive walls of Braşov. Both leaders deployed their troops in a single line. Radu Şerban positioned his infantry on the right flank, while most of the cavalry occupied the centre and the left flank. He also kept a detachment of 1,300 Polish cavalry hidden from the sight of the enemy. The Wallachian voivode made the first move and ordered his infantry to attack the left flank of the enemy. The Transylvanians resisted the infantry assault and prepared for a counter-attack. The Wallachian army performed a fake retreat towards the walls of Braşov, giving the impression that they were planning to take cover inside the allied town. Encouraged by their belief in a swift victory, the Transylvanian cavalry pursued the retreating enemy. Some were diverted towards the Wallachian camp, hoping to raid the unprotected belongings of their enemies. While the overconfident Transylvanian army was advancing without caution, Radu Şerban brought in his reserve cavalry, the 1,300 Polish hussars. Their assault was followed by a general counter-attack performed by the rest of his army. Taken by surprise, the army of Gabriel Báthory began to scatter. Many nobles and *hajdú* leaders were captured by the Wallachian army, while the Prince retreated with his remaining troops into the fortified town of Sibiu.[79]

The army of Gabriel Báthory did not perform as well as expected, and suffered both in size and motivation due to his political mistakes. Many of his *hajdú* mercenaries had already left his army and he did not enjoy the full support of Transylvanian estates. Although the battle took place in Transylvania he essentially fought as if in hostile territory because the Saxons of Braşov did not want to share the fate of those in Sibiu. Radu Şerban won this battle because he twice took advantage of the element of surprise. First, he was able to enter Transylvania without the knowledge of his enemy and chose a battleground in the vicinity of an allied town. Second, he kept his best cavalry hidden and used it when the enemy was least expecting it.

Báthory retreated to Sibiu where he was determined to wait for Ottoman reinforcements. In the meantime the army of Sigismund Forgács was marching through Transylvania from the north-west. His soldiers were not welcomed by the locals who still remembered the hardships endured during the previous periods of Habsburg rule. Most of the country was dissatisfied with the tyrant prince but they did not like the Habsburgs either. In the end, Báthory was saved by Ottoman military intervention. The sultan decided to forgive him his previous transgressions, because leaving him on the Transylvanian throne was preferable to losing the country to the Habsburgs.[80]

---

78 Constantin Rezachevici, 'Neobişnuitul drum peste Carpaţi al oştii lui Radu Şerban, înaintea bătăliei de lângă Braşov cu Gabriel Báthory (iulie 1611)', *Cumidava* VIII (1974–1975), pp.119–131.

79 Kraus, *Cronica*, pp.13–14; *Chronicon Fuchsio-Lupino-Oltardinum*, vol. I, pp.244–245; Rosetti, *Istoria artei militare*, p.354.

80 Veress (ed.), *Documente*, vol. VIII, p.206.

Sigismund Forgács and Radu Șerban decided to retreat from Transylvania because they were no match for the larger Ottoman force. Gabriel Báthory did not give up on his hostile policy and continued his civil war against the Estates. Brașov and Sighișoara refused to recognise his authority and kept their gates closed. The ranks of the rebels continued to swell, as many nobles left the entourage of the Prince, fearing the unpredictability of his reactions. Among them was Gabriel Bethlen, a Transylvanian noble who fled to Istanbul and convinced the sultan that he was a better candidate for the throne. Gabriel Báthory was assassinated by his own soldiers in 1613 thus ending a despotic reign that endangered the very existence of the young Transylvanian Principality.

Conclusion

During the second half of the sixteenth century, Transylvania underwent a complex process of transition from voivodeship to principality. A former province within the Hungarian Kingdom, Transylvania was gradually transformed into a distinct and autonomous state. The change of political status did not bring radical modifications in terms of institutional and administrative organisation. The social and ethnic composition of the region remained mostly unchanged. The country was ruled by a voivode, who later acquired the title of prince, and who was elected by the representatives of the Estates with the approval of the Ottomans. The three Estates (Nobles, Saxons and Székely) sent their representatives to the regular meetings of the Diet. Together with the ruling prince, they made the most important decisions regarding the future of the country. From this point of view Transylvania can be considered an elective monarchy, similar to the Polish-Lithuanian Commonwealth.

An early modern state could not survive without an army, one of its fundamental institutions. Transylvania was no exception and its rulers made constant efforts to improve the military organisation of the country. The composition of the army reflected the complex social structure of the region, with its various groups and classes, each with its own privileges and obligations. Noble levies, peasant militias, Saxon infantry detachments, Székely cavalry and infantry troops and various smaller groups of tax-exempted, semi-professional soldiers were mustered to defend the country from internal and external threats. Most of them performed military service in order to maintain their privileged status although occasionally they also received wages. In addition, the army of the court (the guard of the prince) and the resident garrisons of the main fiscal fortifications, received regular wages and were slowly transforming into a professional body within the Transylvanian military framework.

The performance of Transylvanian soldiers on the battlefield is hard to assess because during this period the country was often divided between those who favoured the Habsburgs and those who were content with the status quo of remaining an Ottoman vassal. In many military campaigns, Transylvanian factions fought on both sides. Nevertheless, contemporary sources offer precious details that are helpful in distinguishing the character of warfare in this east-central European region. One of the most striking features is, without a doubt, the importance of cavalry. Most of the county nobility, the Székely elite and a large proportion of the court army fought on horseback. Under Ottoman influence, sixteenth century Transylvanian horsemen gave up on most of their heavy defensive armour. Some elements of plate and even chainmail were still in use but compared to the fifteenth century, mounted soldiers were lighter, favouring speed and mobility. Such cavalry troops were very efficient in border raids and skirmishes, but were of little use during sieges. In pitched battles, Transylvanian cavalry relied mostly on the speed of their charge and the force of impact, and were usually positioned in the centre of the battle line. This became a serious disadvantage in battles where they faced heavier cavalry (Silesian and Walloon cuirassiers) or when they were effectively flanked by enemy cavalry or infantry.

Infantry warfare was greatly influenced by the spread of gunpowder weapons. The borderland *hajdús*, the infantry of Saxon towns, the guardsmen and even some of the peasants recruited in the county militias were armed with firearms. Their equipment was completed by close combat weapons like sabres, axes, spears and scythes, but they usually lacked defensive equipment. In pitched battles, infantry was often deployed on the flanks and assumed a defensive stance around field artillery. This light infantry formations were excellent in ranged combat but were vulnerable to enemy cavalry charges.

Transylvania had a stable network of fortresses and fortified towns. Its most vulnerable region was the western border, situated in the vicinity of both Habsburg Hungary and the Ottoman Empire. This was the region where most fortifications were concentrated. In the second half of the sixteenth century the defensive system of the country was significantly improved by the spread of bastioned fortifications. This was one of the most important early modern innovation that had reached this part of Europe and had a significant impact on the manner of waging war. Sieges were among the most important military operations during this period and their outcomes had long lasting political and economic consequences. The new principles of military architecture (the bastioned fortification) and the development of gunpowder weapons secured an important advantage for those who defended fortifications. As we have seen in the previous chapters, most sieges in which the Transylvanian army was involved ended with the defenders being victorious. Fortifications were rarely taken by force and when they were eventually conquered it was because the garrisons surrendered for want of supplies.

The organisation of Transylvanian armies and their performance on the battlefield reflects the changes that occurred in the art of war in the beginning of early modern European history. The first seven decades of the Principality of Transylvanian (1541–1613) were marked by a process of transition from medieval military traditions to early modern military innovations. Although it was a small state, always in the shadows of its greater neighbours, the Ottomans and the Habsburgs, Transylvania managed to maintain its autonomous status, its political survival ensured by both diplomatic and military means.

Colour Plate Commentaries

Front cover. Mounted soldier from the court army (guard) of Prince Sigismund Báthory/*Hajdú* soldier from the western borderlands of Transylvania during the Long Turkish War (1591–1606)
The guard of the prince (*aulae militia/aulae exercitus*) consisted of cavalry and infantry detachments that performed regular military service at court. Their main role was to protect the ruler of Transylvania but they also participated in most campaigns and battles. Most of those who served at court were locals but foreign mercenaries were also present, especially Polish and Italians. The cavalry of the court grew in size towards the end of the sixteenth century. During the Long Turkish War (1591–1606), Prince Sigismund Báthory had 2,067 mounted soldiers in his guard. Their equipment, weapons and fighting style were similar to that of the other Transylvanian nobles. They wore breast plates, helmets (*sisak*/*zischagge* type) and asymmetric shields as defensive equipment. The most common offensive weapons were lances, sabres, and *hegyestőr* swords. The *hajdús* lived in borderlands of Hungary and Transylvania. They were initially cattle herders and traders who became very proficient in irregular warfare as the Ottoman threat advanced towards their territories. Their numbers grew steadily towards the end of the sixteenth century and were employed by both the Habsburg Kings of Hungary and the rulers of Transylvania. The most important phase in their history was the anti-Habsburg rebellion of Stephen Bocskai (1604–1606), when they gained privileged status. Most *hajdús* fought as infantry armed with arquebuses and close combat weapons like sabres and axes.

Plate A. Mounted Transylvanian noble and a conscripted peasant (second half of the sixteenth century)
Most Transylvanian nobles performed military service on horseback. The tradition of the noble insurrection, a general levy of the nobility, was inherited from before the partition of the Hungarian Kingdom. Nobles were organised in detachments based on the county of residence. Many attended military campaigns accompanied by small retinues, which included armed servants but also a specific number of conscripted peasants based on the size of their estates. Nobles were usually armed with lances, sabres, maces, and a long sword called *hegyestőr*. Defensive equipment was lighter compared to previous centuries. Most nobles continued to wear breast plates (even chain mail) and steel helmets (the most common were the *sisak* type). Peasant militias were an auxiliary element of the Transylvanian army and were

mustered only in exceptional situations. Some of the conscripted peasants were armed with gunpowder weapons but the vast majority relied on simple, close combat weapons like hunting spears and axes.

Plate B. Mounted Székely *lófő* (early seventeenth century)

Inhabiting the eastern and south-eastern borderlands of Transylvania, the Székely had a long tradition of horse breeding and were renowned for their riding skills. The elite of the Székely community, the so-called leaders (*lófő*), made excellent light cavalry detachments. Armed with lances, long swords (*hegyestőr*) and sabres, the Székely cavalry was usually deployed in the centre of the battle line. Like the county nobility, the Székely *lófő* gave up on heavy defensive equipment in favour of speed and mobility. Nevertheless, during the second half of the sixteenth century and the beginning of the seventeenth century, sources indicate that they continued to use some elements of defensive equipment like shields, plate or chain mail.

Plate C. Saxon Black Guard from the town of Sibiu and a field cannon (second half of the sixteenth century)

The towns of the Saxons were the largest and most prosperous urban settlements in Transylvania. As one of the three political estates of the country, they had to provide detachments of infantry for the Transylvanian army. Most of them were armed with gunpowder weapons (arquebuses) and were designated as *pedites pixidarios*. During the Long Turkish War (1591–1606) the soldiers from Sibiu wore black clothes. In time it became their distinctive colour. In addition, the Saxons provided a large proportion of the field and siege artillery for the Transylvanian army.

Plate D. Guardsman (*drabant*) from the garrison of a western border fortification in Transylvania (second half of the sixteenth century)

Transylvania was defended by an extensive network of fortifications. Most of them were positioned on its western edges, where the territories of the Principality were divided from Ottoman and Habsburg lands. Fortresses, especially those situated on the fiscal estate, were defended by small permanent garrisons and groups of semi-privileged soldiers living in nearby villages. The term guardsman (*drabant/darabont*) was used to designate both types of soldiers. According to Giovanni Andrea Gromo, an Italian mercenary captain who served at the court of John Sigismund Szapolyai in 1564, guardsmen (*drabanti*) were equipped with arquebuses, spears and sabres and their main role was to guard the gates of fortifications.

Plate E. German *landesknecht* from the army of Giovanni Battista Castaldo (1551–1553)

In 1551, General Giovanni Baptista Castaldo brought an army of foreign mercenaries to Transylvania in order to enforce the Habsburg rule and to repel Ottoman attacks. The bulk of his army consisted of *landesknechte*. One regiment of about 3,000 men was led by Count Felix de Arco and entered Transylvania during the summer. A second regiment, recruited in southern Germany and Bohemia, commanded by Colonel Andrew Brandis, joined the Habsburg forces during the siege of Lipova, in November 1551. The *landesknechte* were armed with long pikes, arquebuses and other close combat weapons like the *katzbalger* short swords. Although they had proven their proficiency on many European battlefields they had a hard time fighting the Ottomans and enduring the harsh Transylvanian winter.

Plate F. Spanish arquebusier from the army of Giovanni Battista Castaldo (1551–1553)

In 1551, the Habsburg army in Transylvania was reinforced by a strong contingent of Spanish mercenaries. Their leader was Bernardo Villela de Aldana, *Maestro de Campo* of the Naples *tercio*. He arrived in Hungary in 1548 with 1,400 men. Three years later he joined General Castaldo in Transylvania, with at least 1,200 soldiers. Spanish arquebusiers proved their worth during the two sieges of Timișoara (1551 and 1552). However, their overall performance was reduced by the lack of wages and supplies. They were also involved in several conflicts with the local population over the price of food and religious matters.

Plate G. Wallachian *curtean* from the army of Michael the Brave in Transylvania (1599–1600)

During the first phase of the Long Turkish War, Transylvania, Wallachia and Moldavia rebelled against the Ottomans and joined the Holy League. The ruler of Wallachia, Michael the Brave was initially a trusted ally of Sigismund Báthory and cooperated efficiently, especially during the autumn campaign of 1595. In 1599, after the battle of Șelimbăr, he also became ruler of Transylvania. His army consisted of local troops and various groups of foreign mercenaries. According to Transylvanian chronicler Wolfgang Bethlen, his best cavalry was formed by a group of semi-privileged soldiers who served as guards of the court – *curteni* (*praetorianum aequitatum quos illi Kurtanos vocant*). Their weapons and equipment were rather similar to that of Transylvanian nobles and consisted of wing-shaped asymmetric shields (their use was widely spread in south-eastern Europe), lances, maces, and sabres.

Plate H. Silesian cuirassier in the army of Giorgio Basta (early seventeenth century)

The cuirassiers, also referred to as Silesian heavy cavalry in Transylvania, were among the best troops sent by the Habsburgs to fight in Transylvania during the Long Turkish War (1591–1606). A large detachment of Silesian heavy cavalry (1,500) wearing black armour participated in the Wallachian campaign of 1595. Several companies of cuirassiers joined the garrison of Oradea fortress before the siege of 1598. Giorgio Basta, the Habsburg commander sent to Transylvania in 1600, relied on his cuirassiers for the most daring manoeuvres. They played a decisive role in the battle of Mirăslău (18 September 1600), where they performed a faked retreat and then counter-attacked the lighter cavalry of Michael the Brave. Cuirassiers wore full plate armour, and their offensive weapons were two pistols and a heavy sword.

Bibliography

Archival Sources

Magyar Nemzeti Levéltár OrszágosLevéltára (MNL OL), Budapest, F 7 Armales

MNL OL,F 15, Kolozsmonostori Konvent Országos Levéltára – Protocolla, libri regi et stilionaria

MNL OL, E 156 – a., Urbaria et Conscriptiones

Magyar Tudományos Akadémia Könyvtára, Kézirattár, Budapest, Ms. 4178/3, Endre Veress, *Arcélek Erdély viharos multjábol, Castaldo tábornok Erdélyben (1551–1553)*

Magyar Tudományos Akadémia Könyvtára, Kézirattár, Budapest, Ms. 439/11, Veress Andrei, *Erdély és magyarországi kisebb történeti müvek, Geszthy Ferenc várkapitány c. értekezéshez kiegészitések*

Österreichisches Staatsarchiv, Haus-, Hof- und Staatsarchiv, Vienna, Hungarica, Algemeine Akten

Serviciul Judeţean al Arhivelor Naţionale Sibiu, România, (SJAN Sibiu), Socoteli consulare, nr. 87

Edited Sources

Ardeleanu, Ion et al. (eds), *Mihai Viteazul în conştiinţa europeană: Documente externe* (Bucureşti: Editura Academiei Republicii Socialiste România, 1982)

Basilius, Leonardus, 'Naratio De Rebus Transylvanicis (1599–1604)', Radu Constantinescu *Lupta pentru unitate naţională a Ţărilor Române 1590–1630. Documente externe* (Bucureşti: Direcţia Generală a Arhivelor Statului, Institutul de Istorie 'Nicolae Iorga', 1981)

de Bethlen, Wolffgangi, *Historia de rebus Transsylvanicis*, vol. I–VI (Cibinii: Typis et sumptibus Martinii Hochmeister, 1783–1792)

Beccari da Sacile alla Minerva, Bernardino, *La rotta che ha datta il Serenissimo Prencipe di Transilvania &c. a'i Turchi e Tartari sotto Temesuar alli 17. Di Giugno 1596* (Roma: Nicolo Mutii, MDXCVI)

Beccari da Sacile alla Minerva, Bernardino, *Ragguaglio di tutto l'assedio di Temesvar Fino all levata del Serenissimo Prencipe di Transilvania da quella piazza, Dove s'intendono tre notabili fattioni di Sua Altezza contra i Turchi, et Tartari, Et in particolare la morte del Tartaro Cane pe mano dell'Altezza Sua, & l'acquisto delle sue bagaglie, & della preda che haveva fatta. Seguita a di 19. Giugno 1596* (Roma: Nicolo Mutii, 1596)

Chronicon Fuchsio-Lupino-Oltardinum sive annales Hungarici et Transsilvanici, vol. I, ed. Josephus Trausch (Coronae, 1847)

Corpus Juris Hungarici seu Decretum Generale Inclyti Regni Hungariae Partiumque eidem Annexarum (Budae, 1822)

Crăciun, Ioachim (ed.), *Cronicarul Szamosközy şi însemnările lui privitoare la români 1566–1608* (Cluj: Institutul de Arte Grafice Ardealul, 1928)

Crăciun, Ioachim (ed.), 'Dietele Transilvaniei ţinute sub domnia lui Mihaiu Viteazul (1599–1600)', *Anuarul Institutului de Istorie Naţională Cluj*, VII (1936–1938), pp.620–640

Crăciun, Ioachim (ed.), 'Scrisoarea lui Petru Pellérdi privitoare la ajutorul dat de Sigismund Báthory lui Mihaiu Viteazul în campania din 1595', *Anuarul Institutului de Istorie Naţională*, VI (1931–1935), pp.494–502

Diaconescu, Marius (ed.), *Izvoare de antroponimie şi demografie istorică. Conscripţiile cetăţii Sătmar din 1569–1570* (Cluj-Napoca: Editura Mega, 2012)

Döry, Ferenc, Bónis, György (eds), *Decreta Regni Hungariae*, vol. II (Budapest: Akadémia Kiadó, 1989)

Dudik, Beda, 'Rödern Menyhért császári tábornagy tudósítasa Nagy-Várad 1598-iki ostromoltatásáról', *Történelmi tár*, 1 (1878), pp.101–116

Feneşan, Cristina, 'Codex Vindobonensis Palatinus 7803, eine wenig bekannte quelle über die eroberung von Lipova durch die Habsburger (1551)', *Revue des Études Sud-Est Européennes*, XVIII:1 (1980), pp.14–25

Ghymesi Forgách, Ferencz, *Magyar Historiaja: 1540–1572*, Fidél Majer (ed.), *Monumenta Hungariae Historica, Scriptores*, vol. XVI (Pest, 1866)

Gromo, Giovannandrea, *Compendio di tutto il regno posseduto dal re Giovanni Transilvano et di tutte le cose notabili d'esso regno (Sec. XVI)*, ed. Aurel Decei (Alba Iulia: Tip. 'Alba', 1945)

Guboglu, Mihail, Ali Mehmet, Mustafa (eds), *Cronici turceşti privind Ţările Române*, vol. I (Bucureşti: Editura Academiei R.S.R., 1966)

Hegyi, Ödön, 'Székely Antal tudósítása a Hadadi csatáról', *Történelmi Tár* (1900), pp.142–144

degli Hortensii, Ascanio Centorio, *Comentarii della guerra di Transilvania* (Vinegia: Appresso Gabriel Giolito de' Ferrari, 1565)

Gróf Illésházy István nádor Följegyzései 1592–1603, Gábor Kazinczy (ed.), *Monumenta Hungariae Historica, Scriptores*, VII (Pest, 1863)

de Hurmuzaki, Eudoxiu (ed.), *Documente privitoare la Istoria Românilor*, vol. II/4 (Bucureşti: Academia Română şi Ministerul Cultelor şi Instrucţiunii Publice, 1894)

Iorga, Nicolae, *Documente nouă, în mare parte româneşti, relative la Petru Şchiopul şi Mihai Viteazul* (Bucureşti: Institutul de Arte Grafice Carol Göbl, 1898)

Kraus, Georg, *Cronica Transilvaniei 1608–1665*, G. Duzinchevici, E. Reus-Mîrza (eds) (Bucureşti: Editura Academiei Republicii Populare Române, 1965)

Memorialul lui Nagy Szabó Ferencz din Târgu Mureş (1580–1658), Ştefania Gáll Mihăilescu (ed.) (Bucureşti, 1993)

Meteş, Ştefan, *Vieaţa agrară, economică a românilor din Ardeal şi Ungaria. Documente contemporane 1508–1820*, vol. I (Bucureşti: Tipografia 'România Nouă' Th. Voinea, 1921)

Miles, Mathias, *Siebenlmrgischer Würg-Engel* (Hermannstadt, 1670)

Szilágyi, Sándor (ed.), *Monumenta Comitialia Regni Transilvaniae*, vol. I–XXI (Budapest: Magyar Tudományos Akad. Könyvkiadó Hivatala, 1875–1898)

Szabó, Károly (ed.), *Székely Oklevéltár*, vol. II, (Cluj: A Magyar történelmi társulat kolozsvári bizottsága, 1876)

Szilágyi, Sándor, (ed.), 'Szamosközy István történeti maradványai 1566–1603', vol. I–IV, Monumenta Hungariae Historica 2, Scriptores 28 (Budapest: Magyar Tudományos Akadémia, 1876–1880)

Veress, Endre, *A történetíró Báthory István király* (Cluj-Kolozsvár: Minerva, 1933)

Veress, Andrei (ed.), *Báthory István erdélyi fejedelem és lengyel király levelezése*, vol. II (1576–1586) (Koloszvár: Erdélyi Tudományos Intézet, 1944)

Veress, Andrei (ed.), *Documente privitoare la istoria Ardealului, Moldovei şi Ţării Româneşti, Acte şi scrisori*, vol. I–XI (Bucureşti, 1929–1939)

Monographs and Articles

Abrudan Paul, Sontag Fritz, 'Sistemul de apărare al cetății Sibiului în secolele XV și XVI –expresie a concepției războiului popular', *Studii și Materiale de Muzeografie și Istorie Militară*, 7–8 (1974–1975), pp.121–140

Anghel, Gheorghe, *Cetăți medievale din Transilvania* (București: Editura Meridiane, 1972)

Ágoston, Gábor, 'Behind the Turkish war machine: gunpowder technology and war industry in the Ottoman Empire, 1450–1700', Brett D. Steele, Tamera Dorland, *The Heirs of Archimedes: Science and the Art of War through the Age of Enlightenment* (Cambridge Massachusetts: MIT Press, 2005), pp.102–133

Ardelean, Florin Nicolae, 'Evoluția funcției de căpitan general în Transilvania la sfârșitul secolului al XVI–lea șiîn prima jumătate a secolului al XVII–lea', *Banatica*, 28 (2018), pp.561–582

Ardelean, Florin Nicolae, 'Mercenarii străini și inovațiile militare moderne timpurii în Europa Central-Răsăriteană. Armata lui Castaldo în Transilvania și Banat', *Banatica* 25 (2015), p.41

Ardelean, Florin Nicolae, 'Military Leadership in the Transylvanian Principality. The Captain General in the second half of the sixteenth century', *Banatica*, 26–2 (2016), pp.337–349

Ardelean, Florin Nicolae, 'On the Foreign Mercenaries and Early Modern Military Innovations in East Central Europe. The Army Castaldo in Transylvania and the Banat 1551–1553', in György Bujdosné Pap, Ingrid Fejér, Ágota H. Szilasi (eds), *Mozgó Frontvonalak. Háború és diplomácia a várháborúk időszakában 1552–1568*, *Studia Agriensia*, 35 (Eger: Dobó István Vármúzeum, 2017), pp.117–128

Ardelean, Florin Nicolae, *Organizarea militară în principatul Transilvaniei (1541–1691): Comitate și domenii fiscale* (Cluj-Napoca: Academia Română. Centrul de Studii Transilvane, 2019)

Ardelean, Florin Nicolae, 'Pecunia nervus belli. The Saxon University in Transylvania and its Contribution to the Military Campaign of 1566–1567', in Zoltan Iusztin (ed.), Politics and Society in the Central and South-Eastern Europe (thirteenth–sixteenth centuries) (Cluj-Napoca: Editura Mega, 2019), pp.215–222

Bagi, Zoltán Péter, 'Giorgio Basta: a short summary of a career', in Krisztián Csaplár-Degovics (ed.), *These were hard times for Skanderbeg, but he had an ally, the Hungarian Hunyadi: Episodes in Albanian–Hungarian Historical Contacts* (Budapest: Research Centre for the Humanities – Hungarian Academy of Sciences, 2019), pp.35–67

Bak, János M., 'Politics, Society and Defence in Medieval and Early Modern Hungary', in Béla K. Király, János M. Bak (eds), *From Hunyadi to Rákoczi: War and Society in Late Medieval and Early Modern Hungary* (New York: Columbia University Press, 1982), pp.1–23

Balás, Margit, *A váradi kapitánság története* (Nagyvárad: Láng József Könyvnyomdája, 1917)

Barany, Attila, 'King Sigismund of Luxemburg and the preparations for the Hungarian crusading host of Nicopolis (1386–396)', in Daniel Baloup, Manuel Sánchez, Martínez (eds), *Partir en croisade à la fin de Moyen Âge. Financement et logistique* (Toulouse: Presses universitaires du Midi, 2015), pp.153–178

Borosy, András, 'The Militia Portalis in Hungary before 1526', in János M. Bak, Béla K. Király (eds), *From Hunyadi to Rakoczi. War and Society in Late Medieval and Early Modern Hungary* (New York: Columbia University Press, 1982), p.63–80

Burai, Adalbert, 'Despre cetatea de tip italian din Satu Mare', *Studii și Comunicări. Satu Mare* I (1969), pp.143–160

Costea, Ionuț, 'Social structures', in Ioan-Aurel Pop, Thomas Nägler, András Magyari (eds), *The History of Transylvania*, vol. II (Cluj-Napoca: Center for Transylvanian Studies. Romanian Cultural Institute, 2009)

Costea, Ionuț, *Solam virtutem et nomen bonum. Nobilitate, Etnie, Regionalism în Transilvania Princiară* (Cluj-Napoca: Editura Argonaut, 2005)

Cîmpeanu, Liviu, 'Consecinţele războiului asupra populaţiei civile: cazul luptelor din Transilvania în toamna anului 1600, după căderea lui Mihai Viteazul', *Anuarul Institutului de Cercetări Socio-Umane Sibiu*, vol. XXIII (2016), pp.25–33

Cîmpeanu, Liviu, 'Domnul fie lăudat [...] turcii au predat cetatea': Cucerirea Lipovei Otomane de către Transilvăneni în august 1595', *Historia Urbana*, XXVI (2018), pp.97–111

Cîmpeanu, Liviu, 'Liga nobiliară de la Turda şi revoluţia' Transilvaniei împotriva lui Mihai Vodă (1–18 septembrie 1600)', *Anuarul Institutului de Cercetări Socio-Umane Sibiu*, vol. XXIV (2017), pp.41–63

Cîmpeanu, Liviu, 'Obligaţii militare şi ordine de mobilizare a oraşelor săseşti din Transilvania la sfârşitul evului mediu', *Historia Urbana*, XXVII (2019), pp.123–144

Cîmpeanu, Liviu, 'Organizarea militară a Braşovului până la sfârşitul secolului al XV-lea', Vasile Ciobanu, Dan Dumitru Iacob (eds) *Studii de istorie a oraşelor: in honorem Paul Niedermaier* (Bucureşti: Editura Academiei Române; Brăila: Editura Istros a Muzeului Brăilei 'Carol I', 2017, pp.336–360

Cîmpeanu, Liviu, 'The Royal Habsburg Arsenal in Sibiu (Hermannstadt, Nagyszeben) under the rule of Queen Isabella', in Ágnes Máté, Teréz Oborni, *Isabella Jagiellon Queen of Hungary (1539–1559)* (Budapest: Akadémia Kiadó, 2020), pp.257–273

Cîmpeanu, Liviu, *Universitatea Saxonă din Transilvania şi districtele româneşti aflate sub jurisdicţia ei în evul mediu şi epoca modern* (Târgu Mureş: Editura Nico, 2014)

Cristea, Ovidiu, 'A Second Front: Wallachia and the "Long War" against the Turks', Gábor Kárman, Radu G. Păun (eds), *Europe and the Ottoman World. Exchanges and Conflicts (sixteenth and seventeenth centuries)* (Istanbul: The Isis Press, 2013), pp.13–27

Czimer, Károly, 'Temesvár megvétele 1551–1552' I–III, *Hadtörténelmi Közlemények*, VI (1893), pp.15–71, 196–229, 303–376

D'Ayala, Mariano, 'Vita din Giambattista Castaldo famosissimo guerriero del secolo XVI', *Archivio Storico Italiano*, V:I (Firenze, 1867), pp.86–124

Deschmann, Alajos, 'Huszt vára – A Máramarosi sóbányák őre', *Műemlékvédelem*, 35:3 (1991), pp.156–164

Domokos, György, 'Egy Itáliai várfundáló mester Magyarországon a XVI. század második felében: Ottavio Baldigara élete és tevékenyesége', *Hadtörténelmi Közlemények* (4) (1998), pp.767–856

Dörner, Anton, 'Power Structure', in Ioan-Aurel Pop, Thomas Nägler, András Magyari (eds), *The History of Transylvania*, vol. II (Cluj-Napoca: Center for Transylvanian Studies. Romanian Cultural Institute, 2009)

Engel, Pál, *Regatul Sfântului Ştefan: Istoria Ungariei medievale 895–1526* (Cluj-Napoca: Editura Mega, 2006)

Hermann Fabini, *Universul cetăţilor bisericeşti din Transilvania* (Sibiu: Editura Monumenta, 2009)

Feneşan, Cristina, 'Din premisele luptei antiotomane a Ţărilor Române în vremea lui Mihai Viteazul. Mişcările populare din 1594 în eialetul Timişoarei', *Anuarul Institutului de Istorie şi Arheologie Cluj-Napoca*, XXVII, (1985–1986), pp.100–116

Feneşan, Cristina, 'Le statut de dépendance de la principauté de Transilvanié envers la Porte en 1541', *Revue des études sud-est européennes*, XXXVII–XXXVIII (1999–2000), pp.79–91

Feneşan, Cristina, 'Problema instaurării dominaţiei otomane asupra Banatului Lugojului şi Caransebeşului', Banatica, IV (1977), pp.223–238

Feneşan, Cristina, *Vilayetul Timişoara (1552–1716)* (Timişoara: Editura Ariergarda, 2014)

Gemil, Tasin, *Romanians and Ottomans in the XIVth–XVIth centuries* (Bucureşti: Editura Enciclopedică, 2009)

Ghezzo, Márta A., *Epic Songs of Sixteenth–Century Hungary* (Budapest: Akadémiai Kiadó, 1989)

Ghitta, Ovidiu, 'Biserica Ortodoxă din Transilvania', in Ioan-Aurel Pop, Thomas Nägler, András Magyari (eds), *Istoria Transilvaniei*, vol. II (Cluj-Napoca: Institutul Cultural Român. Centrul de Studii Transilvane, 2005)

Glück, Eugen, 'Contribuții cu privire la istoricul cetății de la Ineu', Ziridava, XIII (1981), pp.131–147

Goldenberg, Samuel, *Clujul în sec. XVI: Producția și schimbul de mărfuri* (Cluj: Editura Academiei Republicii Populare Române, 1958)

Gorun, Gheorghe, 'Fortificații bihorene în lupta pentru apărarea autonomiei Transilvaniei', *Muzeul Național*, V (1981), pp.165–169

Groza, Liviu, 'Cetatea Caransebeș – câteva precizări cronologice', *Bantica*, 12–2 (1993), pp.89–99

Hegyi, Klára, *A török hódoltság várai és várkatonasága*, vol. III (Budapest: História: MTA Történettudományi Intézete, 2007)

Held, Joseph, 'Military Reform in Early Fifteenth Century Hungary', *East European Quarterly*, XI: 2 (1977), pp.129–139

Hossu, Valer, *Nobilimea Chioarului* (Baia Mare: Biblioteca Județeană 'Petre Dulfu', 2003)

Kalmár, János, *Régi magyar fegyverek* (Budapest: Natura, 1971)

Kálnoky, Nathalie, 'L'organization militaire de la nation sicule à la fin du Moyen Âge', in Hervé Coutau-Bégarie, Ferenc Tóth (eds) *La pensée militaire hongroise à travers les siècles* (Paris: Economica, 2011)

Keul, István, *Early Modern Religious Communities in East-Central Europe: Ethnic Diversity, Denominational Plurality and Corporative Politics in the Principality of Transylvania (1526–1691)* (Leiden, Boston: Brill, 2009)

Komáromy, András, 'A Mezőkeresztesi csata 1596-ban', *Hadtörténelmi Közlemények*, V (1892), pp.278–298

Komáromy, András, 'Az 1607-iki hajdúlázadás történetéhez', *Hadtörténelmi Közlemények*, IV (1891), pp.226–233

Korpás, Zoltán, 'Lo que no figura en 'La Expedición': El motín del tercio viejo de Bernardo Aldana en Hungría, 1553', *Libros de la Corte* 21:12 (2020), pp.63–91

Kovács, András, 'Gyulafehérvár, site of the Transylvanian princely court in the sixteenth century', Gyöngy Kovács Kiss (ed.), *Studies in the History of early modern Transylvania* (New York: Columbia University Press, 2011), pp.319–358

Kovács, András, 'Szilágysomlyó vára a 16. Században', *Dolgozatok az Erdélyi Múzeum érem- és régiségtárából*, VIII (2013), pp.95–106

Kovács, Klára, *Cetatea din Gherla. Răspândirea fortificației în sistem bastionar italian în Transilvania* (PhD Thesis) (Cluj-Napoca: Babeș-Bolyai University, 2009)

Kovács, Klára, 'Fortress-Building in 16th-Century Transylvania. The Recruitment of Labour Force', *Transylvanian Review*, Vol. XXI, Supplement No. 2 (2012), pp.163–181

Kovács, P. Klára, 'Planimetria cetății bastionare de la Satu Mare în context european', *Ars Transsilvaniae* XIX (2009), pp.27–35

Kovács, Tibor S., *Huszár-fegyverek a 15–17. Században* (Budapest: Martin Opitz Kiadó, 2010)

Kozák-Kígyóssy, Szabolcs László, 'Fegyverkészítő kézműiparosok és céhek a késő középkori Nagyszebenben', *Hadtörténelmi Közlemények* 3 (2018), pp.539–560

Kubinyi, András, 'Hungary's Power Factions and the Turkish Threat in the Jagiellonian Period (1490–1526)', in István Zombori (ed.), *Fight against the Turk in Central-Europe in the first half of the sixteenth century* (Budapest, 2004), pp.115–147

Lemajić, Nenad, 'The Serbian Population of the Banat and the Western Mureș Basin in the fifteenth and sixteenth Centuries (and its Local and Military Leaders)', in Đura Hardi (ed.), *The Cultural and Historical Heritage of Vojvodina in the Context of Classical and Medieval Studies* (Novi Sad: Faculty of Philosophy, 2015), pp.205–223

Lukinich, Imre, *Erdély területi változásai a török hódítás korában, 1541–1711* (Budapest: Kiadja a Magyar Tudományos Akadémia, 1918)

Lukinich, Imre, 'La jeunesse d'Etienne Báthory', in Adrien de Divéky (ed.), *Etienne Báthory: roi de Pologne, prince de Transylvanie* (Cracow, 1935), pp.23–34

Lupescu Makó, Mária, *Talem fecisset testamentum ... Testamente nobiliare din Transilvania medievală* (Cluj-Napoca: Argonaut, 2011)

Lukács, Antal, *Țara Făgărașului în Evul Mediu (secolele XIII–XVI)* (București: Editura Enciclopedică, 1999)

Madgearu, Alexandru, *The Romanians in the Anonymous Gesta Hungarorum: Truth and Fiction* (Cluj-Napoca: Romanian Cultural Institute, 2005)

Magina, Adrian, 'Conscripția și inventarul bunurilor cetății Ineu în anul 1605', *Banatica* 21 (2011), pp.90–104

Magina, Adrian, 'Le long voyage vers la terre promise: Les migrations serbes en banat (XVe–XVIe siècles)', in Florin Nicolae Ardelean, Cristopher Nicholson, Johannes Preiser-Kapeller (eds), *Between Worlds: The Age of the Jagiellonians* (Frankfurt am Main: Peter Lang Edition, 2013), pp.129–140

Magina, Livia, *Instituția judelui sătesc în Principatul Transilvaniei* (Cluj-Napoca: Editura Mega, 2014)

Makkai, László, László Makkai, 'István Bocskai's Insurrectionary Army', Béla K. Király, János M. Bak (eds), *From Hunyadi to Rakoczi. War and Society in Late Medieval and Early Modern Hungary* (New York: Columbia University Press, 1982), pp.275–297

Makkai, László, László Makkai, 'The first period of the Principality of Transylvania (1526–1606)', in Béla Köpeczi (ed.), *History of Transylvania*, vol. I (New York: Columbia University Press, 2001), pp.593–797

Makkai, László, László Makkai, 'Transylvania in the Medieval Hungarian Kingdom', in Béla Köpeczi (ed.), *History of Transylvania*, vol. I, (New York: Columbia University Press, 2001), pp.311–590

Marta, Doru, *Cetatea Oradiei: De la începuturi până sfârșitul secolului al XVII–lea* (Oradea, 2013)

Nägler, Thomas, 'Transylvania between 900 and 1300', in Ioan-Aurel Pop, Thomas Nägler (eds), *The History of Transylvania* (Cluj-Napoca: Center for Transylvanian Studies. Romanian Cultural Institute, 2005), vol. I, pp.199–233

Oborni, Teréz, 'Fráter György szervitorainak és familiárisainak jegyzéke a Castaldo-Kódexben, 1552', Fons, 25: 4 (2018), pp.435–451

Oborni, Teréz, 'State and governance in the Principality of Transylvania', *Hungarian Studies*, 27:2 (2013), pp.313–324

Pakucs-Willcocks, Mária, *Sibiul veacului al XVI–lea: rânduirea unui oraș transilvănean* (București: Humanitas, 2018)

Pálffy, Géza, *The Kingdom of Hungary and the Habsburg Monarchy in the Sixteenth Century* (Boulder Colorado: Social Science Monographs, 2009)

Pálosfalvi, Tamás, *From Nicopolis to Mohács: a history of Ottoman-Hungarian warfare, 1389–1526* (Leiden; Boston: Brill, 2018)

Panaitescu, Petre P., *Mihai Viteazul* (București: Fundația Regele Carol I, 1936)

Papo, Adriano, Nemeth Papo, Gizella, *Frate GiorgioMartinuzzi: Cardinale, soldato e statista dalmata agli albori del Principato di Transilvania* (Canterano: Arcane editrice, 2017)

Péter, Katalin, 'The Golden Age of the Principality (1606–1660)', in László Makkai, Zoltán Szász (eds) *History of Transylvania*, vol. II (New York: Columbia University Press, 2002)

Pop, Ioan-Aurel, 'Ștefan Mailat și țara (cu cetatea) Făgărașului', *Mediaevalia Transilvanica*, II:2 (1998), pp.239–244

Prodan, David, 'Boieri şi vecini în Ţara Făgăraşului în sec. XVI–XVII', in *Din istoria Transilvaniei. Studii şi evocări* (Bucureşti: Editura Enciclopedică, 1991), pp.9–159

Idem, *Iobăgia în Transilvania în secolul al XVI–lea*, vol. I–II (Bucureşti, Editura Academiei, 1967–1968)

Rady, Martyn, *Nobility, Land and Service in Medieval Hungary* (Basingstoke: Palgrave, 2000)

Rezachevici, Constantin, 'Viaţa politică în primele trei decenii ale secolului al XVII–lea. Epoca lui Radu Şerban, a Movileştilor şi a lui Gabriel Bethlen', Virgil Cândea (ed.), *Istoria Românilor*, vol. V (Bucureşti: Editura Enciclopedică, 2003), pp.35–105

Rosetti, Radu R., *Istoria artei militare a românilor până la mijlocul veacului al XVII–lea* (Bucureşti: Corint, 2003)

Roşu, Felicia, *Elective Monarchy in Transylvania and Poland-Lithuania, 1569–1587* (Oxford University Press, 2017)

Rusu, Adrian A., *Castelarea carpatică: Fortificaţiile şi cetăţile din Transilvania şi teritoriile învecinate (sec. XIII–XIV)* (Cluj Napoca: Editura Mega, 2005)

Attila Sunkó, 'Az erdélyi fejedelmi testőrség archontológiája a XVI. Században', *Fons*, 2 (1994), pp.186–214

Attila Sunkó, 'Az erdélyi fejedelmek udvari hadai a 16. Században', *Levéltári Közlemények*, 69:1–2 (1998), pp.99–131

Sebestyén, Gheorghe, 'Cronologia cetăţii Gherla (II)', *Studii şi Materiale de Istorie Medie*, XVII (1999), pp.223–237

Szabó, János B., Somogy, Győző, *Az Erdélyi fejedelemség hadserege* (Budapest: Zrinyi Kiadó, 1996)

Szabó, János B., 'A székelyek katonai szerpe Erdélyben a mohácsi csatától a Habsburg uralom megszilárdulásáig (1526–1709)', in József Nagy (ed.), *A Határvédelem évszázadai Székelyföldön: Csíkszék és a Gyimesek vidéke. Szerkesztette és a jegyzékeket összeállította* (Szépvíz, 2018), pp.101–153

Szabó, János B., 'Splendid Isolation? The Military Cooperation of the Principality of Transylvania with the Ottoman Empire (1571–1688) in the Mirror of the Hungarian Historiography's Dilemmas', in Gábor Kármán, Lovro Kunčević, (ed.), *The European Tributary States of the Ottoman Empire in the Sixteenth and Seventeenth Centuries* (Leiden and Boston: Brill, 2013), pp.301–339

Szabó, János B. 'The Army of the Szapolyai Family during the Reign of John Szapolyai and John Sigismund (Baronial, Voivodal and Royal Troops, 1510–1571)', Pál Fodor and Szabolcs Varga (eds), *A Forgotten Hungarian Royal Dynasty: The Szapolyais* (Budapest: Research Center for Humanities, 2020), pp.207–239

Szádeczky, Louis, 'L'election d'Etienne Báthory au trône de Pologne', in Adrien de Divéky (ed.), *Etienne Báthory: roi de Pologne, prince de Transylvanie* (Cracow, 1935), pp.82–105

Szegedi, Edith, 'The birth and evolution of the Principality of Transylvania', in Ioan-Aurel Pop, Thomas Nägler, András Magyari (eds), *The History of Transylvania*, vol. II (Cluj-Napoca: Center for Transylvanian Studies. Romanian Cultural Institute, 2009)

Szilágyi, Sándor, 'Békes Gáspár versengése Báthori Istvánnal (1571–1575)', *Erdélyi Múzeum-Egyesület Évkönyve*, I (1859–1861), pp.107–115

Tătar, Octavian, 'Tratatul de la Speyer (1570) dintre Maximilian al II–lea şi Ioan Sigismund Zápolya şi statutul politico-teritorial al Transilvaniei pe plan european', *Annales Universitatis Apulensis. Historica*, 7 (2003), pp.191–197

Trócsányi, Zsolt, *Erdély központi kormányzata. 1540–1690* (Budapest: Akadémiai Kiadó, 1980)

Trócsányi, Zsolt, 'Rákóczi Zsigmond (Egy dinasztia születése)', *A Debreceni Déri Múzeum Évkönyve 1978* (1979), pp.57–111

Trócsányi, Zsolt, *Törvényalkotás az Erdélyi Fejedelemségben* (Budapest: Gondolat, 2005)

Țigău, Dragoș Lucian, 'Between Ephemerality and Fiction. Addenda to the History of the Bans of Caransebes and Lugoj', Banatica, 26:2 (2016), pp.351–367

Țiplic, Ioan Marian, *Bresle și arme în Transilvania (secolele XVI–XVI)* (București: Editura Militară, 2009)

Ursuțiu, Liviu, *Domeniul Ghurghiu (1652–1706): Urbarii inventare și socoteli economice* (Cluj-Napoca: Editura Argonaut, 2007)

Vekov, Károly, *Structuri juridico-militare și sociale la secui în evul mediu* (Cluj-Napoca: Editura Studium, 2003)

Veress, Andrei, 'Campania creștinilor în contra lui Sinan Pașa din 1595', *Academia Română. Memoriile secțiunii istorice*, IV: 3 (1925), pp.66–148

Virovecz, Nándor, *Balassa Menyhárt élete és a kora újkori magyar politikai kultúra* (PhD Thesis) (Budapest: Eötvös Loránd University, 2017)

Whelan, Mark, 'Pasquale da Sorgo and the Second Battle of Kosovo (1448): A Translation', *Slavonic and East European Review*, 94:1 (2016), pp.126–145

Wolf, Rudolf, 'Cetatea Șimleului. Schiță monografică', *Acta Musei Porolissensis*, V (1981), pp.395–409